P9-DNB-019

ANECDOTES OF
Music and Musicians

ANECDOTES OF
Music and Musicians

By HELEN L. KAUFMANN

EDITED UNDER THE SUPERVISION OF
THOMAS K. SCHERMAN
Director, Little Orchestra Society

Grosset & Dunlap
PUBLISHERS
NEW YORK

©COPYRIGHT 1948 BY
HELEN L. KAUFMANN

Under the title:
THE LITTLE BOOK OF MUSIC ANECDOTES

ALL RIGHTS RESERVED

©1960 BY GROSSET & DUNLAP

PRINTED IN THE UNITED STATES
OF AMERICA

CONTENTS

Contents

◇◇◇◇◇◇◇◇◇◇◇◇◇◇◇◇◇◇◇◇◇◇◇◇◇◇◇◇◇

ALL FOR LOVE

THE HANDSOME YOUNG MUSICIAN, Alessandro
Stradella, was by no means displeased when
he was commissioned by a wealthy Venetian
nobleman to teach singing to the nobleman's
lady-love, Hortensia. Indeed, though this
was in the cloak-and-dagger days of the early
seventeenth century, he tempted Providence
by promptly falling in love with the lady, who
returned the compliment. The enamoured
couple determined to run away together from
their "protector," regardless of consequences.
They went first to visit Naples, Stradella's
birthplace and then, with an uneasy sense of
guilt and impending doom, to Rome.

Their premonition was correct. Two as-
sassins had been engaged by the deserted nobleman to wreak vengeance on the lovers. On
an evening when Stradella's oratorio was to be
performed in the Church of St. John Lateran
in Rome, with Stradella singing the principal
solo role, the two hirelings planned to waylay
him in the street after the performance. They
entered the church at five o'clock, in order to
keep an eye on their intended victim. How-

ever, they were so moved by the beauty of the music and Stradella's part in it, that their resolve faltered. Outside the church, instead of meeting him with a dagger, they spoke soft words to him, told him of the plot against his life and of the large reward they had been promised for murdering him, and doubtless had a bottle of wine with him as a reward for their musical good judgment and for their restraint regarding his liquidation.

Thus warned, the young couple then went to Turin, where they placed themselves under the protection of the powerful Duchess of Savoy. Hortensia entered a convent to await the Church's permission to marry, and the young man became the Duchess's chapel-master. Meanwhile, two more emissaries from the implacable nobleman had been set on his trail. As he walked on the city ramparts one evening, he was brutally stabbed. The perpetrators fled, leaving him for dead. But miraculously he recovered and, as soon as possible, he and Hortensia were married.

Their married life was too brief. Business called him to Genoa. He had written an opera for that city, and, with Hortensia, he went to supervise its performance. They were in their bed, after a glorious musical triumph, when two men forced their way into their bedroom and brutally stabbed and killed them both.

THEY THAT GO DOWN TO
THE SEA IN SHIPS

KING CHARLES II of England was a monarch
who took his fun where he found it—and he
found it in many forms. At one time a yacht
of his own seemed a highly desirable toy, so
he had one built according to royal specifica-
tions for his royal pleasure. As soon as it was
pronounced ready to go, he invited a group
of friends and courtiers to accompany him
on a cruise. They sailed away in high spirits,
all set to eat, drink and make merry. Their
destination was the Kentish coast. They had
been out only a short while when they ran
into a terrific storm. What with thunder and
lightning, raging winds and high seas, and an
untried boat, the danger of shipwreck loomed
menacingly close. The king and courtiers,
with the captain and all hands, remained on
deck praying for deliverance. No-one dared
to go below. Apparently their prayers were
heard, for the storm abated. The ship put
about, and all landed thankfully in London.

Gostling, a bass singer in the choir of the

Chapel Royal, was one of the party. The experience made a profound impression upon him. He was deeply grateful that his king's life had been spared, not to mention his own, and cast about for a way of expressing his gratitude in his own language, song. As he was seeking an appropriate text in the Bible, he came across the lines:

They that go down to the sea in ships,
These men see the Works of the Lord,
And his wonders in the deep.
For at his word the stormy wind ariseth
Which lifteth up the waves thereof.
They are carried up to Heaven
And down again to the deep.
Their soul melteth away because of trouble,
They reel to and fro, and stagger like a drunken
    man,
And are at their wits' end.
So when they cry unto the Lord in their
    trouble
He delivereth them out of their distress.
For he maketh the storm to cease
So that the waves thereof are still.
Then are they glad because they are at rest,
And so he bringeth them unto the haven where
    they would be.
O that man would praise the Lord for his good-
    ness,

And declare the wonders that he doth for the
    children of men,
That they would exalt him also in the Congre-
    gregation of the People,
And praise him in the seat of the Elders.
O praise the Lord for his goodness,
And declare the wonders that he doth for the
    children of men.

Gostling took the words to Henry Purcell,
organist of the Chapel Royal and composer-
in-ordinary to the king, and asked him to set

them to music. Purcell obliged with an
anthem which has become world-famous.
Since he wrote it for Gostling, who was a basso
profondo, his melody contained a low D which
is a terror to the ordinary bass singer. But
Gostling took it in his stride. He sang a first
performance of the anthem in the Chapel
Royal, in a thanksgiving service attended by
all the members of the sailing party—except
the monarch responsible for it!

Contents

Contents

Contents

Contents

LEARNING A NEW LANGUAGE

It is my deep-seated belief that music is a language, with its own rules of grammar and structure, its own wide vocabulary and certainly its own literature expressed in many distinct and personal styles, each of which has its own strict set of regulations. It is as foreign a language to most of us on first exposure as are French, Russian, or Japanese.

Of course none of us would presume to expose ourselves to everyday communication in French, Russian, or Japanese, let alone to read their great creative masterpieces in the original, without at least basic knowledge of the rudiments of the native language.

In just the same way, I feel it is equally presumptuous of us to expose ourselves to a concert of live music or a good recording of a great symphony or opera and expect to receive any message from them, without having first acquainted ourselves with the basic rudiments of the "language" in which they are written. We must, in other words, be active listeners, bringing to the music knowledge of the composer's style and an understanding of musical form.

But how can we learn this foreign language, with all its strange illusive meanings? We do not need the amount of intensive training required of a composer or performer. We need only enough knowledge to understand, to a degree, what they are both *saying* to us. And the more we become familiar with the language, the more depths will we discover in their speech.

The first door to this sanctuary is that of learning the basic vocabulary and grammar—the knowledge of the different basic styles of music; a casual acquaintance with the instruments with which it is performed;

a more intimate acquaintance with the lives and working habits of the great composers and interpreters of the past; a sense of *historical* perspective of music, (*why*, for instance, Bach used the instruments and the forms which he did, instead of using the instruments and forms of, say, Tchaikovsky or Gershwin); an appreciation of the different *forms* in which most of the masterpieces were written (so that, on hearing a sonata for the first time, we can recognize its themes and know when to expect their repetition); an idea of why and how folk songs and jazz have had such an important influence on music of the great composers; and last but not least, an acquaintance with the stories of the songs, and of the tone poems, and of the operas, to which we will be exposed.

This modest series of books is merely intended as a key to this first door. It is merely an introduction to the fascinating but complex vocabulary and rules of grammar and syntax of the great musical language. If the books succeed in stimulating some readers to further investigation into the rich resources of that language, then they will have served their purpose.

THOMAS SCHERMAN

VERDICT—GUILTY!

DR. THOMAS ARNE, an English composer of the 1770's, sat in his study in London one day, puffing at his pipe, and surveying with quiet satisfaction the music he was writing for Shakespeare's *Tempest*. Deeply engrossed, he hummed to himself the lines "Where the bee sucks, there suck I, In a cowslip's bell I lie," and found them good. As he nodded his sat- isfaction, a knock sounded on his door, fol- lowed by another, more assertive. Annoyed at the interruption, he at first failed to answer, hoping that the unwelcome intruder would de- part. Then, with a sigh, he recalled that he had promised to audition two young singers who aspired to an appearance in one of the operas Handel was then producing at Covent Garden. He had made the appointment and he was in duty bound to keep it. Suppressing his irritation, he called resignedly "Come in." Two young men entered together, like Twee- dledum and Tweedledee. "Good day, Sir. We have an appointment," they spoke as one. "Good day. Yes, I know." "May we sing

for you, then?" "Yes, yes, but one at a time,
please. I will accompany you at the spinet."

Hardly waiting for Dr. Arne to place the
music on the rack and seat himself at his instrument, the first young man struck an attitude, cleared his throat and plunged. The
sounds he emitted were ear-piercing but he
sang on to the raucous end. Without a word
to him, the good Doctor turned to the second.

"Will you sing now?" he asked. Nervous but
determined to do or die, the second victim

burst into a difficult aria with many brilliant
passages which he failed utterly to deliver.
His effort was a complete fiasco.

The Doctor turned to the first performer.
"You are without doubt the worst singer I
ever in my life have heard," he said quietly.
"Then," cried the second, "*I* win." "You!"
thundered Dr. Arne. "*You* can't sing at all!"
And without another word, he bowed them
both out.

BACH'S UNAPPRECIATED TRIBUTE

LEOPOLD, PRINCE OF CÖTHEN, was giving a party. It was a somewhat special event, for he was not in his royal palace at Cöthen, but in Carlsbad, famous health resort. True, he had come to Carlsbad that May of 1718, to drink the waters, not to amuse himself, but that did not prevent him from filling his salon with guests for the musicales he was so fond of giving. Nor did it induce him to part, even temporarily, from Johann Sebastian Bach, his musical man-of-all-work. No, Bach and several members of the court orchestra, plus a cembalo with three servants to care for it, traveled with him. For the prince loved music above all things and himself often played the violin in the chamber orchestra conducted by Bach.

He liked, moreover, to display to his friends the unusual treasure he had in his Kapellmeister. When Bach first arrived in Cöthen, in 1717, he found very little instrumental

music in the prince's library. He found plenty
of good players—violinists, trumpeters, flutists,
bassoonists, oboeists, and performers on the
viola da gamba and the clavier—but very little for them to play. He speedily set about
remedying this lack, and thanks to his industry,
many new works for chamber orchestra, besides sonatas and suites for one or more instruments, soon were placed on the music racks.
His output was enormous thanks to his
prince's constant encouragement.

Now, in the silk-hung salon in Carlsbad,
Bach at the cembalo and a quintet of players
discoursed sweet music, just as though they
had been at home. One gentleman in the
audience showed special interest, and while
the other guests sipped punch and chatted, he
clapped Bach on the shoulder with some such
words as "Bully for you, old chap." He was
Christian Ludwig, Margrave of Brandenburg, a well-known patron of the arts. He
had his own orchestra, and the kind of income
that enabled him to commission works whenever the spirit moved him. He followed his
words of praise with kindly remarks which the
composer construed as a commission. Soon
after his return to Cöthen, then, Bach set to
work on the *Concerts pour Plusieurs Instruments*,
later known as the *Brandenburg Concertos*.

Two years later, he sent them to Branden-

burg in time for the young Margrave's birthday on March 24, 1721, with a letter couched
in the humblest terms.

"*Monseigneur,*

*Two years ago, when I had the honor of playing
before your Royal Highness, I experienced your
condescending interest in the insignificant musical
talents with which heaven has gifted me, and understood your Royal Highness's gracious willingness to
accept some pieces of my composition.   In accordance
with that condescending command, I take the liberty
to present my most humble duty to your Royal Highness in these Concerti for various instruments, begging your Highness not to judge them by the standards
of your own refined and delicate taste, but to seek in
them rather the expression of my profound respect and
obedience.   In conclusion, Monseigneur, I most
respectfully beg your Royal Highness to continue your
gracious favor toward me, and to be assured that
there is nothing I so much desire as to employ myself
more worthily in your service.*

*With the utmost fervor, Monseigneur, I subscribe
myself,*

*Your Royal Highness's most humble and most
obedient servant,*

JEAN SEBASTIAN BACH."

Coethen, 24 March, 1721.

But princes are gifted with conveniently
short memories, and Christian Ludwig had

apparently forgotten the Carlsbad incident. At any rate, no reply from him is on record. He did not have the concertos included when his works were catalogued. He probably never even allowed his orchestra to play them for him—to his shame be it spoken—for, when examined years later, the manuscript still had an unread look. It remained obscurely tucked away until after his death in 1734. Then it was put up for sale with a job lot of unwanted works, and passed from owner to owner until it came to rest in the Royal Library, in Berlin.

In 1850, a century after Bach's death, the Brandenburg Concertos were published and played! Ironically, they brought to the name of Brandenburg a lustre created by none of its reigning princes, but by their "humble and obedient servant," Johann Sebastian Bach.

◆◆◆◆◆◆◆◆◆◆◆◆◆◆◆◆◆◆◆◆◆◆◆◆◆◆◆◆◆

DOMENICO SCARLATTI
AND HIS *CAT'S FUGUE*

DOMENICO SCARLATTI sat in the garden of his
villa in Naples one morning in the early
1700's, gazing at the blue sky, stroking his pet
cat at intervals, content with the world save
for an elusive musical theme which came to
him, only to disappear before he could capture
it. His meditations were interrupted by the
arrival of his young pupil, Hasse, who called
from the music-room, "Master, I am here for
my lesson. "One moment," called Scarlatti.
"Please be seated." He remained in the garden, hoping to fix in his mind the theme of his
new composition before starting to teach.

Hasse had no mind to be seated. He roamed
restlessly about the room looking at the pic-
tures, handling small objects, whistling impatiently.

Meanwhile his dog, Truelove, kept a baleful
eye on Scarlatti's cat, a privileged character.
As if to mock him, the cat brushed daintily
past the harp, sending forth a sweet jangle,

then jumped on to the harpsichord, whence she surveyed her enemy. Hasse, for the fun of it, lifted the dog and placed him on the cat's back, saying "Here, give your guest a nice ride." Enraged, the cat raced over the keyboard, trying to shake off her burden, and mewing frantically for her master to come to the rescue. Finally, the dog fell off with a crash, and the cat, much relieved, executed a dance of triumph on the keyboard.

"You have found it, cat," called Scarlatti. "That is the theme I've been looking for." He hurried into the room. "You will have to excuse me today," he said to Hasse. "No lesson. I must write this music at once while it is fresh in my mind. Come tomorrow instead." The young man, nothing loath, took himself off. When he returned the following day, Scarlatti showed him the manuscript and played for him on the harpsichord the now famous *Cat's Fugue*.

THE HORRORS OF
PERSECUTION

GLUCK'S OPERA *Armide* was produced at a time
when people quarreled even more violently
over their music than over their politics.
Gluck, beloved teacher of Marie Antoinette,
had already stirred up a small hornet's nest
by writing operas in a fashion new to his time.
He subordinated vocal gymnastics to musical
effects, and enriched the orchestral accompaniment. And most important—he tried to
make the personages of the opera behave like
human beings, who sang as they felt, instead
of like lay-figures delivering set declamatory
solos. After writing *Armide*, he said happily,
"I have discovered the means of making the
personages speak so that you know at once,
from their mode of expression, when Armide
is speaking, when the confidante, etc." This
was revolutionary. Gluck was the "modern
composer" of his day.

Like modern composers from time im-
memorial, he had a fight on his hands. The

opposition to him crystallized in the person of an Italian composer named Piccini, now remembered chiefly for the controversy with Gluck. Piccini came to Paris. His opera *Roland*, written in the "good old-fashioned style," was produced at the same time as *Armide* (1777), bringing to a focus the dissensions already existing between the Gluckists and the Piccinists.

The ambassador from Naples, Marchese Carraciolo, loyal to his countryman, Piccini, caballed insidiously against Gluck at the court

of Marie Antoinette. He wined and dined
most of Paris to gain supporters for Piccini.
He set the courtiers against one another and
won the favor of King Louis and his circle.
At the opera, the Courtiers in the Coin du Roi
(King's corner) and the Coin de la Reine
(Queen's corner) faced each other glaring
and scowling. Between the acts, they took
issue on the merits of their respective favorites
and sometimes they came to blows, gleefully
egged on by the Marchese. That worthy
ambassador also inspired critical articles by
Marmontel, de la Harpe, and other distinguished writers, all designed to discredit
Gluck.

When the persecution took written form,
Gluck rose nobly to the occasion. A delight-
fully ironic letter from him in answer to an
article by M. de la Harpe has been preserved.
De la Harpe criticized an aria sung by Armide
as being "too full of fury." Gluck wrote in
reply: "Sir, if some blockhead should say
to me 'Pray remember that Armide in a state
of fury should not express herself like Armide
enamored,' I should reply 'Sir, I do not wish
to offend the ear of M. de la Harpe; I do not
wish to adhere to nature, but rather to *em-
bellish* it; instead of making Armide utter
cries of anguish, I wish her to *enchant* you. In
her despair, Armide should sing an air . .so

regular and methodical and at the same time so tender that the most delicate "petite maîtresse" may listen to it without the smallest shock to the nerves.' " He likewise offered (ironically) to rewrite the whole libretto, beg ging de la Harpe to suggest a "rhymer" who would insert a couple of arias into every scene, while Gluck for his part would banish from the orchestra the kettledrums and trumpets, leaving only oboes, French horns, and muted violins. In the course of his letter, he remarked, with mock modesty, "I was confounded to find that you had learned more of my art in some hours of reflection than I had done after having exercised it for forty years."

Thanks to all the preliminary dissension, the house was packed to the doors for the première of *Armide*. So closely were members of the audience crowded together that one of them, when requested by an usher to remove his hat, retorted, "*You* take it off; I can't move my arms." The audience found the opera so moving that they wept and beat their breasts and at the end left the opera-house, as one observer described it, "with hair disordered and clothes soaked." When the storm of criticism broke afterward, an enthusiast consoled Gluck, saying "Sir, you are fortunate to enjoy the horrors of persecution; all the greatest geniuses have followed that path."

RAMEAU'S TWENTY YEARS' WAR

THE OPERATIC DÉBUT in Paris of Jean Philippe Rameau in 1733 initiated a controversy which continued, with bitter violence, for over twenty years. When his opera *Hippolyte et Aricie* was produced, Rameau was already fifty years old. He had devoted much of his life to exploring and evolving a philosophic science of harmony, a somewhat grey occupation, operatically speaking. He himself was grey and dour, no glowing young exponent of music-drama. Not outwardly, that is. But inwardly, he had cherished for years his dream of writing operas, a dream finally realized through his finding an "angel" in the person of the wealthy courtier, La Pouplinière.

Lully, who up to that time had been un-disputed master of the French opera, had been dead for fifty years when *Hippolyte et Aricie* was performed. Yet his admirers, calling themselves the Lullistes, rallied to his memory at the first hint that a possible rival had ap-peared on the scene. With all their force, they aligned themselves against the Ramistes, derisively calling them "ramoneurs" (chimney sweeps). They resented the more complex harmonies in Rameau's music, the "bizarre" songs, the expansion of the overture which introduced the opera—all the innovations, in fact, which differentiated Rameau's opera from the ultra-classical operas of Lully (himself decried in his day for departures from the classical model). They sabotaged the production of *Hippolyte* wherever they could. They bribed actors and musicians to play hookey under the pretence of illness. They wrote diatribes in the public press, misquoting and deriding Rameau. He, for his part, wrote in perplexity, "I have always considered Lully a great master. . . . How long will people continue to listen to the supposed remarks which are constantly being attributed to me, while they refuse even to give me credit for acts of which anyone may hold the proof in his hand?"

Against him were the soundly entrenched conservatives, the older generation, his personal enemies and his jealous competitors. His own group of friends met often at La Pouplinière's, planning their campaign. Diderot, the French author and editor, remarked, "The ignorant and barbarous all stand up for do mi do sol (Lully). The young and the virtuosi are for do re mi fa sol la si do do do (Rameau). And men of taste think highly of both." Unfortunately, there were not enough men of taste.

Hippolyte et Aricie had more than thirty performances, and the general public liked it well, despite the wrangling of the so-called connoisseurs. Rameau doggedly overcame the difficulties which beset each performance. *Les Indes Galantes*, in 1735, proved even more popular. Then Lully's *Persée* was produced, in reprisal. Its success was moderate. Rameau countered with *Castor et Pollux* in 1737. This was somewhat coolly received, and the Lullistes said "Aha, we told you so!" *Atys* restored him to public favor but brought him no nearer to the Lullistes' good graces. Voltaire, who wrote the libretto for Rameau's opera, *La Princesse de Navarre*, remarked that "Rameau had a party against him that would have liked to exterminate him." And all because he employed harmonies with which they were unfamiliar and dared to write melodies somewhat more complex than those to which they were accustomed.

Eventually, after Rameau had put in twenty years at hard labor on one opera after another, the opposition of the Lullistes abated and he was permitted for a short while to bask in the sunshine of success. But another rival appeared. Pergolesi's opera, *La Serva Padrona*, was brought from Italy, and produced at the French court. King Louis XV and his followers were enchanted and hailed Italian opera with gusty enthusiasm. Again Rameau's loyal followers took a stand, this time on the national issue of French versus Italian music. But Rameau himself recognized the unmistakable charm of Pergolesi's opera. He said wistfully, "If I were twenty years younger, I would go to Italy and take Pergolesi for my model. But after sixty one cannot change; experience points plainly enough to the best course but the mind refuses to obey." Thus gracefully he abdicated, relinquishing, in part at least, the disputed leadership he had won with so much effort.

TARTINI, DEVIL'S DISCIPLE

A MONK'S CELL is not the place where one would expect to find a disciple of the Devil, much less the Devil himself. But the bare little cubicle in a monastery near Padua which harbored Giuseppe Tartini in 1713 is said to have witnessed a historic meeting between the two. An arrestingly brilliant composition for the violin was the result.

Tartini had arrived at the monastery two years previously in a somewhat battered condition. His refusal either to study for the priesthood or to become a lawyer had angered his family. His secret marriage to the niece of the Bishop of Padua, when discovered, had so enraged that gentleman that Tartini had had to flee for his life. The monks had given him asylum, and he had utilized the isolation and calm of the religious life to apply himself to his violin, which he loved better than anything in the world.

One night, he fell into a doze on his hard pallet, and dreamed that the Devil appeared to him, complete with horns and tail. Tartini readily made a pact with him, promising his immortal soul in return for the gratification of his wishes. In his dream, he asked for many things, one more fantastic than another, and all were given to him. Finally, he handed his violin to His Satanic Majesty, requesting a tune. The Devil complied, and played a sonata so strangely beautiful that it caused Tartini to swoon in his sleep. When he awoke, the vision had vanished.

He seized his instrument and feverishly tried to reproduce what he had heard, but at this point the miracle ceased to operate. He played a sonata, but it was not the one he had heard in his dream and, try as he would, he could only recapture a small part of it. Nevertheless, the piece he did write proved to be one of his best, a diabolically difficult virtuoso work. He called it *The Devil's Trill* in compliment to its inspiration.

SKULLDUGGERY

JOSEF HAYDN DIED in Vienna on May 31,
1809, and was duly laid to rest in the
Hundsthurm Cemetery. Some time after the
funeral, as night was falling, his friend Karl
Rosenbaum visited the grave, and stayed to
pray beside it. Nobody else was in the cemetery at the time.

In 1820, a full eleven years later, it occurred to Prince Esterhazy that since Josef
Haydn had served the Esterhazys long and
faithfully, his remains should be honorably
interred with theirs in the ancestral castle at
Eisenstadt. The Prince ordered the body exhumed. To his and everyone's horror, the
head was missing. It was nowhere to be
found. "Vandalism," cried the Prince. A
search was instituted; everyone who had been
at the simple funeral was questioned. Rosenbaum's friendship for Haydn was well known,
and the fact that he was an amateur phre-
nologist was also mentioned. Then someone
remembered seeing him leave the cemetery on

that long-ago evening with a round package wrapped in newspaper under his arm.

The police questioned him. They searched his house from cellar to attic. Only one room they did not enter. Frau Rosenbaum lay ill in bed, and her husband begged that her privacy be respected. He had good reason for his plea, for Haydn's skull was hidden beneath her mattress; her illness was feigned. The police, of course went away empty-handed. But Prince Esterhazy was so sure that Rosenbaum knew more than he was telling, that he offered to pay him well for the skull or information leading to its whereabouts. At last, Rosenbaum sent him a skull that he said was Haydn's, and it was interred in Eisenstadt with Haydn's bones.

In most unprincely fashion, Prince Nicholas Esterhazy II then refused to pay up, whereupon Rosenbaum informed him that he hadn't sent Haydn's skull at all, but had substituted another. Despite subsequent threats and pleas, Rosenbaum kept the genuine skull in his own possession. But before his death, he confessed the whole story, and bequeathed Haydn's skull to the Gesellschaft der Musikfreunde in Vienna. There it remained, to the immense chagrin of the Esterhazy family.

A LULLABY WITH THIRTY VARIATIONS

BEFORE THE DAYS of barbiturates, rich men with insomnia resorted to other ways of wooing sleep. A large dose of music was considered good medicine and if a resident musician could be retained to administer it, the patient was as good as cured.

A pupil of J. S. Bach, named Goldberg, was engaged by the wealthy Count Kayserling to act as his soporific. At the count's summons, Goldberg would tiptoe in and play quietly upon the harpsichord in the room adjoining the bedroom. Sometimes he played for hours at a time, improvising when his repertoire was exhausted. Then Kayserling had the idea of having something especially written for him as a sleep-inducer. Goldberg suggested his teacher to do the job. And so arrangements were made with Johann Sebastian Bach. For two hundred ducats in a golden cup, he agreed to produce a piece guaranteed to put any listener to sleep. And in that way, there came into being the magnificent Aria with thirty variations known today as the Goldberg Variations. It not only satisfied Count Kayserling, it also put him to sleep.

But audiences of today gladly stay awake, to follow the infinite contrapuntal variety, to rejoice in the inventiveness and applaud the inspiration of the composer of this "lullaby." Johannes Brahms, playing it on the piano as he wept for his dying mother, said of it, "What music that is! Like oil! Bach has power to soothe troubled hearts."

HALLELUJAH

FOR YEARS it has been customary for audiences to rise and have a seventh-inning stretch when the Hallelujah Chorus from Handel's *Messiah* peals forth from organ and choir. The first time the oratorio was performed in England, people stood up with a great rustle, as though all were moved simultaneously by the same impulse. Handel's admirers—or perhaps his public relations counsel—made much of the incident as an indication of the irresistible power of that mighty chorus, as it might well have been. Ever since then, audiences have risen in unison at that point in the Messiah, obedient to the leadership of the few who think they know the reason.

It was an inconsiderate realist who punctured this romantic story, and supplied a simple explanation which has the ring of truth. He noted that King George and his family had entered the royal box just as the first Hallelujah rang out. Naturally, his subjects rose, and remained standing until he was seated. Their rising at the opening and sitting at the close of the chorus was purely coincidental. "A fig for the irresistible musical urge!" said this observer.

A BLACKSMITH'S GIFT
TO HANDEL

IT IS QUITE A LONG STEP from the clank of hammer on anvil to the delicate tinkle of the harpsichord. But George Friedrich Handel took it with no apparent difficulty. A clumsy, fleshy man in body, he proved as agile as a mountain goat when musical gymnastics were in order.

He was living in England, where he spent most of his life, when chance led him to *The Harmonious Blacksmith*. On the principle, "While in England, do as the English do," he went one day for a long cross-country walk. Just as he reached the small village of Edgware, a deluge of rain descended, and he hastily sought shelter under the nearest roof, which happened to be that of the village smithy. The smith, unaware that his visitor was a distinguished composer, continued to work with no more than a friendly nod. As he worked he sang, and his brawny arms brought the hammer down with a resounding clank in time to his singing.

Handel was struck by the tune, with its ringing, rhythmic accompaniment. He listened with all his ears. When the storm was over he thanked his host warmly, and returned without delay to his own home, hardly waiting to change his wet clothes before writing the smith's tune. At his leisure, he improvised

variations on the harpsichord, and wrote down those that pleased him. He had never hesitated to borrow tunes that he liked, and on this occasion his impulse was rewarded. The air with variations which resulted from his cross-country walk, and which he entitled *The Harmonious Blacksmith*, is one of the most charming of his smaller works.

HAYDN'S
MINUET OF THE OX

ONE DAY, A VISITOR came to call on Papa Haydn in his study in Vienna. He introduced himself as a butcher in the town, who loved music in general and admired Haydn's in particular. In halting accents, he begged a favor. His daughter was shortly to be married. Would Haydn write a minuet for the occasion? Smiling benignly, the composer took a pinch of snuff and told him to return in twenty-four hours. The following day, the minuet was waiting for the fond father.

A few days later, as Haydn again sat at his desk, sounds of music ascended to his study from the street below, and he recognized his minuet. Beneath his balcony, he saw a strange group. A magnificent white ox wreathed in flowers and with gilded horns stood below his window, patient as though listening to the music being played by the orchestra which had followed him. The butcher entered Haydn's study and made a deep bow. He read a prepared speech, in

which he besought the great man to accept
his finest ox in token of his gratitude and his
daughter's.

Haydn could do no less than accept the gift,
and the minuet which prompted it became
known in Vienna as the *Minuet of the Ox*.

HAYDN'S
SURPRISE SYMPHONY

No one loved music more truly than the
Austrian Prince Esterhazy, who maintained
a private orchestra at his castle for over thirty
years and retained Joseph Haydn to conduct
it. But music-lover though he was, he liked
to take a snooze during the concerts over which
Haydn labored so diligently. Perhaps it was
he who originated the time-honored excuse for
concert napping, that he "could listen better
with his eyes closed."

Haydn, however, couldn't help being a little
nettled when a snore punctuated his melodies.
He decided to play a joke on the Prince and
set about preparing it with unusual care. He
invited the Esterhazy family to a very special
concert at which he promised to play a new
symphony.

When all were seated, he began his program
as usual. But he had written into the symphony a long slow movement, that would have
soothed even a chronic insomniac to slumber.
It acted like a charm on the Prince, already

disposed to drowsiness. And then, *Bang!* A sudden noisy chord shattered the murmuring melody. The Prince awoke with such a start that he almost fell from his chair. He slept no more during *that* concert, at least.

Haydn called his joke the *Surprise Symphony.* When he visited London some years later, he used it with equally telling effect on British audiences, dozing in their seats after their heavy dinners of beef and ale. The Bang! never failed to awaken them.

◆◇◆◇◆◇◆◇◆◇◆◇◆◇◆◇◆◇◆◇◆◇◆◇◆◇◆

HAYDN'S
FAREWELL SYMPHONY

THE DAYS AT Esterhazy Castle were growing short, the nights long and cold. It was late autumn and Haydn and his shivering orchestra longed to exchange the bleak country landscape for the warmth and gaiety of Vienna. But their teeth-chattering and shivering were hints that went unheeded. Prince Esterhazy and his family were warm and comfortable in their luxurious quarters on the estate and saw no reason to hasten their return to town.

Haydn had an idea—as usual, a symphonic one. He wrote a symphony with an unexpected ending. In the last movement, the music grew fainter and fainter until it almost faded away. He instructed the players to leave the stage one by one, each as he did so extinguishing the candle over his music stand. At the end only one man was playing and when he too blew out his light and tiptoed away, the stage was left in complete darkness and silence.

Prince Esterhazy saw the point. What is

more, he laughed heartily and applauded
roundly. Perhaps he pulled Haydn's ear and
called him a rascal. But he did relent, and
shortly afterward moved his family, bag and
baggage including the orchestra, to Vienna.

HAYDN'S NATIONAL ANTHEM

WHEN, AT THE HEIGHT of his career, Josef Haydn received a flattering invitation to visit London, it was very difficult for him to make up his mind to go. The very thought made him homesick for Vienna, where every stick and stone, every man, woman and child was dear to him. There is a story to the effect that Salomon, the English manager, had played a sort of London-Bridge tug-of-war with him, offering him every inducement to cross the channel, only to be refused. Then one day the composer came in while Salomon was shaving. He exclaimed aloud at sight of the gleaming English steel razors, which he admired extravagantly. It took only the promise of a similar set of razors for himself to overcome his resistance.

He did go to London, not once but many times, and came to love it dearly. The thing that impressed him most on his first visit was not its fog, nor its bobbies nor omnibuses, nor even Buckingham Palace and the Tower. It was the English national anthem, *God Save the King*, known in the United States as *America*, or

My Country 'Tis of Thee. If the English could summon Deity so passionately to save their king, Haydn saw no reason why the Austrians should not do likewise for their emperor. So he penned an anthem for his own people, *Gott Erhalte Franz den Kaiser* (*God Preserve Franz the Emperor*.) The tune and the sentiment caught on immediately. In 1797 he wrote a string quartet, using as one entire movement the theme of the anthem, to which he added variations. It is known as the Kaiserquartet (Emperor Quartet), and is a most beautiful work.

Some years later, when Haydn lay dying in Vienna, that was the tune he asked to hear. It had a special significance at that time (1809), for Napoleon was bombarding the city, and Austria's fate trembled in the balance. A large cannon-ball had fallen close to Haydn's house, and it was all he could do to reassure his frightened servants. "Don't be afraid," he calmed them. "Don't you know that no harm can befall you while Papa Haydn is here?" He then asked them to carry him to the piano, and very slowly and solemnly he played three times the national anthem he had written. It moved them to tears, yet reassured them. He was carried back to bed, and died there peacefully a few days later, his anthem the last music he was to hear in this world.

A JOYFUL *MISERERE*

WHEN MOZART was in Rome in 1770 on one of his "infant prodigy" tours, he demonstrated his powers in unique fashion. The celebrated *Miserere* by Allegri was to be performed at the Sistine Chapel. To be allowed to hear it was considered a great privilege. To follow with a score was impossible, for no scores were available. It was not published nor known outside the Chapel; to play any part of the music on any but consecrated ground was considered a sacrilege.

The fourteen-year-old boy eagerly sought and obtained admittance to the performance in the Chapel. He listened entranced, his head between his hands, his every faculty concentrated. After the performance, he spoke to no-one but hurried home as though in a trance. He at once went to his desk, seized pen and ink and music-paper, and set himself to the task of writing what he had heard. Overnight, he reproduced the entire score from memory—playing, singing, and writing by turns.

Chancing to meet Christofori, one of the singers, on the grounds of the Academy, Mozart asked him to sing a certain place in the Miserere. Christofori hesitated. The song was forbidden, they were on unhallowed ground, yet he did not like to refuse. Looking cautiously about for possible spies, he deliberately sang the requested phrase in the wrong key. "No, no, that's wrong," Mozart interrupted. "This is the way it goes." And he sang the entire excerpt in the correct key.

A few days later he gave a concert before a brilliant audience. As always his hearers were transported by his playing and called loudly for encores. He seated himself at the harpsichord, struck a few chords and then, carried away by the excitement of the moment, began to sing the *Miserere*, accompanying himself on the harpsichord. When he had finished, there was a stunned silence. His listeners, divided between admiration and fear of the consequences should his temerity come to the ears of the Pope, dared not applaud.

They need not have feared for the Pope, when he heard of the boy's exploit, was deeply impressed by his musicianship. He granted him an audience, in the course of which he uttered no word of reprimand. On the contrary he praised him highly and bestowed on him the knightly Order of the Golden Spur.

DON GIOVANNI,
AN OVERTURE WITH
PUNCH

MOZART HAD TO MEET a dead-line. His opera *Don Giovanni*, on which he had labored long and lovingly with his preferred librettist Da Ponte, was scheduled for a first performance in Prague on Nov. 3, 1787. It was complete, except for the overture. As to that, the composer had three in mind, one in E-Flat Major, one in C Minor, and one in D Major with a slow D Minor introduction. He was never niggardly when it came to ideas. He tried all the overtures on his friends, who rather preferred the D Major. Still he was not quite satisfied, and deferred writing it. When the rehearsals were about finished, the overture was not yet begun.

The impresario, Guardasoni, became edgy, and, although he knew the facility with which Mozart produced, he implored him to get to work. Mozart soothed him, assuring him that everything would be all right. He promised

faithfully that he would write the overture
the afternoon before the dress rehearsal.
Guardasoni accordingly sent a messenger for
it. Mozart was not to be found. He had
gone for a drive with his wife. Resignedly,
the impresario prepared to substitute the
overture to *Idomeneo*, if the worst came to the
worst and nothing else was forthcoming.

When Mozart came gaily home late that
night, he found his friends waiting for him.
They surrounded his carriage, scolding, re-
proaching him. "Let me go. It will be all
right, I promise," he insisted. Dubiously
they dispersed. He went into the house, sat
down at his desk, rumpled his hair, stared at
the blank paper. After a few moments of
this, he said to Constance, "It's no go. I'm
too sleepy. I'll lie down for an hour. Wake
me, please, and have a good strong punch
ready to help me along."

Fully dressed, he flung himself upon the
bed, and in a moment he was sound asleep.
Punctually at the hour's end, Constance went
to awaken him, but he was sleeping so sweetly
she had not the heart to rouse him. She gave
him another full hour's grace, then kissed him
to consciousness. He sat up, rubbed his eyes,
shook himself. "Stay and sit with me," he
begged. So she sat beside him at his desk,
kept his glass filled with punch, sipped some

herself, and told him stories all night long, from nursery tales to Arabian Nights. He smiled and nodded as his pen flew over the paper. Finally, at four in the morning, the work was finished. At seven the copyist arrived to collect it. By seven in the evening, the parts were all copied, ready to be put on the stands, though the ink was still wet, and the sand sprinkled on it hardly dry.

Somehow the story had got around, and when Mozart came out to conduct the orchestra, the house greeted him with loud bravos. He acknowledged the applause, bowing repeatedly. Then, turning to the musicians, he said softly, "Gentlemen, unfortunately we have had no rehearsal. But I know I can rely on you. And so, if you please—!" He lifted his baton. Like a roll of thunder, the first D Minor chord was heard,—the Andante, —the joyous Allegro. When the overture had been played to the end, the storm of applause was deafening. Mozart turned smiling to Guardasoni. "A few notes fell under the music-stands," he said, "but it went excellently anyway. I am greatly obliged to the members of the orchestra."

MOZART'S INCOME TAX

ALTHOUGH THERE WERE no income tax blanks
as such in Mozart's day, people were occasionally called upon to make an accounting,
wherein they signed on the dotted line a statement of their income, their method of earning
it, their employer, and so forth. While Mozart
was employed as chamber composer to Emperor Joseph of Austria—a regrettably niggardly monarch—he was handed such a paper,
with instructions to fill it out. He sat biting
his pen. Named "Wolfgang Gottlieb Mozart," he wrote. Then added happily,
"Changed name to Wolfgang Amadeus Mozart, since it means the same, and sounds
much more musical." At the line which required him to fill in his salary, he knit his
brows, and chewed his pen anew. Reluctantly he wrote, "Eight hundred gulden" (less
than 400 dollars). And under special remarks, he wrote with a bitter scratch of the
pen, "Too much for what I accomplish, too
little for what I *could* accomplish."

MOZART'S *REQUIEM*

As MOZART SAT in his study one day, dejected and ill, cudgeling his brains for a way to pay his debts and take care of the ever-present daily expenses, he heard a knock at the door. Almost before he called "Come in," a grey-cloaked figure stood in his doorway. Without a word, the stranger handed him a letter and immediately withdrew, as though whisked away by magic. Mozart feverishly tore open the missive. It contained an order to write a Requiem Mass as soon as possible, naming his own price. Mozart's sick fancy perceived in the stranger a visitor from another world, come to pronounce his doom, and invite him to compose his own requiem.

Just previous to this, he had contracted with his friend Schikaneder for a comic opera. Schikaneder had shown him the libretto of *The Magic Flute*, and had begged him to see what he could do with it. He had replied "If I do not bring you out of your trouble, and the work is not successful (the producer needed money) you must not blame me, for

I have never written magic music." Here he
was, then, caught between two difficult as-
signments, a bright comedy on the one hand,
and a requiem on the other. Putting the latter determinedly behind him, he climbed into
the coach provided by Schikaneder, and was
whirled away to a little garden pavilion near
the Auf den Wieden Theatre. The change of
scene, and the jolly companionship of the
members of the cast roused him from his depression, and *The Magic Flute*, one of the light-
est and gayest of operas, was completed in a
few weeks.

It was like a final laugh at life, a spurt before the collapse. After the first few performances, which were mildly successful, he returned home, again depressed at what he
felt to be the failure of his efforts, and started
the Requiem, writing with feverish energy.
But death overtook him before the work was
completed. The power of suggestion, added
to severe intestinal fever, proved too much for
him. To the end, he and his wife pretended
to each other that his illness was not fatal, but
both knew the truth.

When Constance learned, after her husband's death, that the visitant had been no
messenger from another world, but simply the
steward of Count Walsegg, she was rightly
indignant at thought of the mental agony suf-

fered by Mozart because of the Count's caprice. He had wished to pass off the Requiem
as his own, and had instructed his steward to
observe all secrecy in delivering the message.
Unwittingly, he had hastened the composer's
end.

◇◇◇◇◇◇◇◇◇◇◇◇◇◇◇◇◇◇◇◇◇◇◇◇◇◇

BEETHOVEN'S FAVORITE SYMPHONY, THE *EROICA*

BEETHOVEN AND THE POET Kuffner sat side by
side on the terrace of the Zur Rose tavern, in
Nussdorf. Beethoven was in the expansive
mood induced by the country, the moonlight,
and an excellent dinner washed down with
good local wine. He feasted his eyes on the
silver stream that rushed by to join the blue
Danube, and gazed upward with satisfaction
at the tall trees arched over his head. Perhaps he thought flittingly of the time he had
refused to occupy a lodging he had rented,
sight unseen, because he found no trees around
it when he went to take possession. He protested, "This house won't do for me. I love
a tree more than man."

His meditations, whatever they were, were
interrupted by an occasional remark from
Kuffner, a great admirer of his music. "Tell
me frankly, Beethoven, which is your favorite
symphony of the eight that you have written?"
asked the poet, after a long pause. "The

Eroica," replied Beethoven decidedly. "I should have guessed the C Minor, No. VII," ventured Kuffner. "No," insisted the composer. "The *Eroica*, Number III."

It is odd that he should have selected, of the eight symphonies he had completed at the time, that which represented one of the major disappointments of his life. He had cherished an enthusiasm for Napoleon, whom he believed destined to become one of the great democratic leaders of all time. He had created the Third Symphony, sub-titled it *Eroica* (Heroic), and had written the name "Bonaparte" in a grand flourish on the title page. The work was completed between 1803 and 1804, Napoleon had himself declared emperor in 1804. When the news was brought to Beethoven, he was aghast. He was too wise to believe that an emperor—even a Napoleon—could long remain true to democractic principles, however vociferous the lip-service rendered. And, as later events proved, he was right.

When the news of Napoleon's accession to the throne was brought to Beethoven, he exclaimed bitterly "Then he's nothing but an ordinary man. Now he'll trample on the rights of men to serve his own ambition; he'll put himself higher than all the others, and turn out a tyrant." Some chroniclers report that Beethoven trod the manuscript of the symphony under foot in his rage. In any event, he at once erased the name of Bonaparte from the title-page, and when the work was published the Italian title stated merely that the symphony was "to celebrate the memory of a great man."

BEETHOVEN'S TRIUMPH

THE VON BREUNINGS were having a musicale. In the little Rhineland town of Bonn, this was an event to be enjoyed. Not only were the Von Breunings intimate with young Ludwig van Beethoven, who played the piano extremely well and composed music besides, but they knew every musician and music-lover in and out of Bonn; knew, too, that musicians love good food and good company. So on this evening, their house was ablaze with lights, their hospitable table laden, their guests many and merry.

The music, too, was of the best. Chamber music,—a sonata, a string quartet, perhaps a trio, started the ball rolling. Then Count Waldstein rapped on the table, and asked the company's attention. He had, he said, brought the manuscript of a piano trio by an anonymous composer. He had not heard it, but it looked to him like a pretty good work, and he wondered if they'd care to try it. He asked Beethoven, who was a good reader, to play the piano part, and two other guests volunteered for the violin and cello.

In an attentive silence, the trio was played, and met with warm approval. The applause was more than polite,—a spontaneous outburst that lasted for several minutes. Afterward, in the buzz of comment, the question most often asked was "Who could have written it?" "Too passionate for Haydn," said one. "Too gloomy for Mozart" replied another. "By a man who thoroughly understands his work" was the general verdict.

At this moment, Count Waldstein took Beethoven's hand and led him forward. "Here you see the composer," he announced. "It is Ludwig van Beethoven, whom you all know." Beethoven's *First Trio*, now so well known and loved, was also his first triumph as a composer.

A SHREWD DEAL

IT ALL DEPENDS upon whose ox is gored. Take for instance the stories of Beethoven's quarrels with publishers, for which his demanding, irascible nature is given all the blame. He apparently needed to put on an act occasionaally, to save himself from exploitation. When he failed to do so he paid the price.

At one time the composer Clementi was in Vienna, representing a firm of English music publishers. Himself a fine composer, he nevertheless drove a hard bargain with his fellow artists. He wrote a gleeful letter, to his employers reporting that "By a little management, and without committing myself, I have at last made a complete conquest of that haughty beauty, Beethoven." It appears that, after several social meetings, Beethoven had so far departed from his usual habit as actually to come to call on Clementi. From him had come the first advances toward better acquaintanceship, which lost him the first round in the duel of wits.

At the first call, Clementi was out. Point

two against Beethoven, who called a second time. Clementi received him only after a long wait, a time-honored tactic in the war of nerves. He flattered Beethoven cleverly,— not too fulsomely, but sufficiently to influence him to bring for inspection all works ready for publication. He was rewarded by having placed in his hands the manuscript of the three great Rasumovsky string quartets, Opus 59; the Fourth Symphony; the Coriolanus Overture; the Violin Concerto; and the Piano Concerto No. IV in G Major—with an apology because nothing more was ready!

Beethoven gave Clementi the sole right to publish these works in England, and received, for seven masterpieces, the sum of two hundred pounds—less than a thousand dollars. He agreed furthermore, for another sixty pounds to compose on order two piano sonatas and a piano fantasia! No wonder Clementi was gleeful about his coup. Even at the prices being paid to successful composers at the time, he had secured a bargain in Beethoveniana.

BEETHOVEN'S SOFTER SIDE

THE BARONESS VON ERTMANN was sunk in melancholy. She had brought several children into the world, only by a tragic fatality to lose them. When the last one was taken from her, she felt that truly nothing and no-one could comfort her. Her friends came, murmuring their sympathy, doing their best to cheer and distract her. She took no heed of them, never raised her eyes from their fixed gaze at the floor. One thing she did notice in spite of her grief. Her good friend Ludwig van Beethoven, who had visited her frequently in happier days, failed now to come to see her. The truth was that so deeply did he feel her loss that he could not bring himself to the point of entering her house of grief to pay the conventional condolence call.

After some days had elapsed, however, he sent her a note begging her to come to see him. She acceded,—since it was Beethoven who asked. When, bowed low in her grief and heavily veiled, she entered his study, he rose, took her hand, and led her to a chair without uttering a word. Then he said gently "We will now talk to each other in tones." Seating himself at the piano, he played for over an hour without stopping. For the first time since her loss, the Baroness's tension relaxed. A sense of peace stole over her. She left the house as silently as she had entered it, but in relating the incident in later years, she said "He told me everything with his music, and at last brought me comfort."

FROM TA-TA-TA TO
SYMPHONY

IT WAS SPRING in Vienna. A laughing stag
party sat at a candle-lit dinner-table in one of
the charming inns for which Vienna is famous.
Count Brunswick, brother of Beethoven's beloved Thérèse, Stephen Breuning, Maelzel the
inventor, and other friends, were giving Beethoven a farewell dinner prior to his departure
for the summer. Though he had stomach
trouble for which his doctor had prescribed
the baths of Carlsbad, no one seeing him at
this moment would have suspected it. He was
in high spirits after putting away an excellent
meal.

During a lull in the gaiety, Maelzel launched
on a description of a gadget he was perfecting,
a mechanical time-keeper. It could be set to
tick beats at different rates of speed, as the
player wished, and would also enable a composer to indicate on his manuscript the tempo
at which he wanted his piece performed.
Maelzel planned to call it a metronome. Beethoven applauded the idea, and character-

istically burst into an improvised song, with a repeated "ta—ta—ta" in imitation of the tick. Soon he had the crowd singing a farewell canon improvised on the spot, using the ta—ta—ta theme. He himself sang a lusty soprano, while Maelzel growled a bass. After the party broke up, he thriftily wrote the theme of the canon in his precious note-book, where he banked musical ideas as they occurred to him.

Not long afterward he started the Symphony No. 8 in F Major, which makes use of this material. He may have made a beginning while traveling. He took a stage-coach for Töplitz via Prague, and in Töplitz met the poet Goethe. It was here that the often-related incident occurred, when Beethoven and Goethe, walking together, met the imperial family coming from the opposite direction. Goethe stopped, took off his hat, and stood respectfully to one side. Beethoven, magnificent democrat, rammed his hat securely on his head and plunged forward, to be greeted affectionately by the Archduke Rudolph, while Goethe stood by unnoticed.

In Töplitz, too, our hero met Amalie Sebald, one of the many girls of his dreams. While drinking the waters, taking the baths, and working on his symphony, he still managed to sandwich in some very warm love-letters to her, which show a sincere and lasting attachment, although like all his beloveds she married somebody else. Some of the most exquisite passages of the symphony he was working on hark back to this romantic interlude.

It was after he arrived at his brother Johann's house in Linz that he set to work in earnest, for he was writing two symphonies at once, No. VII and No. VIII. Not that his two months' stay there was peaceful, far from it! Johann, a bachelor, had a fine big house, presided over by the buxom Thérèse Obermyer as housekeeper. So far, so good. But it was not long before Beethoven, assisted by the gossips of Linz, decided that there was "something rotten in the state of Denmark," or rather in Johann's house. He took a high moral tone with the delinquent, who only laughed. Then he interfered in earnest. He actually reported the immorality of the household to the police and the bishop of the town. They promised to save Johann from himself. Thérèse was to be banished to Vienna if she had not left his bed and board by a specified date. All that Beethoven accomplished by this was to work himself into a rage that was distinctly bad for his health, destroy his own peace of mind, and antagonize Johann, who found himself forced into an immediate and unwelcome marriage with Thérèse. Beethoven bitterly called her the

Queen of the Night, and never forgave her or his brother.

After the marriage, the composer left the house in which he had found so little peace. Yet Symphony No. VIII, produced during these bitter days, has moments that are playful, witty and gay, Beethoven in his "unbuttoned" mood, the mood of the dinner-party. Berlioz wrote about it, "This sort of thing falls entire from heaven into the composer's brain." But it seems rather to have fallen in the form of crumbs from the composer's table, crumbs that fed and satisfied a hungry world of music lovers.

A BARMECIDE FEAST

ONE DAY, Beethoven walked into his favorite restaurant, the Swan, for the hearty midday meal he so greatly relished. He seated himself and rapped on the table for mine host. Nobody came; everyone was occupied elsewhere. Beethoven rapped again, more peremptorily. Still there was no offer of service. While waiting, he drew from his pocket one of the little note-books in which he jotted down musical ideas as they came to him. They were to become one of the most precious heritages that he left, revealing as they did the workings of a genius's mind. At the moment, there was no obvious indication of their value. All that was to be seen was a sober citizen writing in a rather grubby book.

At last a waiter, having disposed of his other clients, came to Beethoven's table and asked him what he would have. Deep in work, Beethoven made no reply. Again the question, again no answer. The waiter knew his man, and decided to leave him in peace until he came out of his musical trance. The composer wrote busily for some time. At last he jumped up, rapped smartly on the table.

"Bring me my bill, please," he ordered loudly. "But you haven't eaten anything," he was told, to his astonishment.

Some years later, the waiter's reply was to be used in quite a different connection. Paderewski, the great pianist, was invited for dinner to the home of a wealthy patron of the arts. After the meal, she led him to the piano, and said coaxingly, "You'll play for us now, won't you?" "But madam, I have eaten so little," was his polite way of refusing to **be** exploited.

PAYMENT DEFERRED

WHEN BEETHOVEN conducted the première of his Ninth Symphony, he had become so deaf that he could not hear the thunder of his music, and was equally impervious to the thunders of applause that rose from the audience. Quite unaware of the tumult, he kept his back turned until a member of the orchestra about-faced him to bow his thanks.

Encouraged by its reception, he decided, a few days later, to dedicate the symphony to His Majesty Friedrich Wilhelm II, the then King of Prussia, who might—who knew—make him some remuneration. After the fashion of the time, he sent with the score a letter couched in the humblest terms. As "a citizen of Bonn," he wrote, he was sending this "trifling token" of his reverence for the king's virtues, and begged his acceptance thereof. The king was graciously pleased to accept the dedication, and in terms as condescending as Beethoven's were humble, he wrote, "In view of the recognized worth of your compositions, I was much pleased at receiving the new work which you have sent me. I thank you for this gift, and send you the accompanying diamond ring as a token of my sincere appreciation."

But Beethoven needed money more than he needed diamonds. He at once took the ring to a jeweler, and offered it for sale. To his chagrin, he learned that the "diamond" was an imitation, worth but a few florins. The prince to whom he saw fit to dedicate what many consider his greatest symphony thought no more of it than to dismiss it with a condescending note and a fake jewel.

TIT FOR TAT

"OUT, YOUNG MAN. You have no business here. Get out." It was Cherubini, the irascible autocrat of the Paris Conservatoire, evicting young Hector Berlioz from its library. They had had an argument, and Cherubini had lost his temper, not an unusual occurrence. When his words failed of their effect, he gave chase. Berlioz jumped nimbly over tables and chairs; Cherubini undignifiedly pursued him. It was almost a knockdown, dragout fight, the result of Cherubini's jealous disapproval of the young composer who refused to abide by the rigid rules of composition as he taught them. Berlioz never forgave or forgot that incident, nor the fact that, as a struggling, starving young composer, he competed for three successive years for the coveted Prix de Rome, and each time it was Cherubini who swayed the judges' decision against him.

Cherubini's opera, *Ali Baba*, was performed in Paris in 1793 or thereabout. The red-haired Berlioz was there, conspicuous as always, and in a front seat. At the end of the first act, he gave a yawn that could be heard all through the house. Turning to his neighbor, he proclaimed audibly, "I'll give twenty francs for *one* idea." In the middle of the second act, he raised his bid, first to forty, then to eighty francs. During the third act, he fidgeted, yawned, shook himself, conversed. Finally, he got up and stalked out. "No," he proclaimed. "It's no use. I give up. I simply am not rich enough."

SPOKEN WITH AUTHORITY

THE SHARP-TONGUED Cherubini was asked to give his opinion of a score of doubtful authorship. It was said to be Méhul's. An obscure composer brought the score to him in person, and waited anxiously for the verdict. Cherubini scanned it rapidly.

"It is not Méhul's," he pronounced. "It is too bad to be his."

"Will you believe me, M. Cherubini, if I tell you that it is mine?" chirped the composer.

"No," flatly countered the old grouch. "It is too good to be yours."

IF FRANZL DOES IT,
IT MUST BE RIGHT

SCHUBERT WAS SHUT into his little room in
Vienna, trying to write music as fast as he could
think it. It was dinnertime, and his good
friends Spaun and Mayrhofer stopped by to
take him out to eat, for they knew that if they
didn't, he would probably forget all about
dinner. They found him pacing up and down,
reading aloud from a volume of Goethe's
poems, his face shining with enthusiasm.
Barely stopping to nod a greeting, he finished
reading the poem, rushed to his table, and
wrote as fast as his pen would move. They
waited just long enough for the ink to dry on
the paper, then went to their favorite café to
try the new composition on the piano. Spaun
and Mayrhofer forgot dinner, were interested,
but puzzled by Schubert's music.

The song tells of a father's ride through the
wild winter night, with his child clasped in
his arms. The child whispers that he sees the
Erlkönig beckoning to him, inviting him in
wheedling tones to go with him. The father
soothes him, telling him that he hears nothing

but the wind in the trees. They ride on. Suddenly, the child utters a sharp cry, sobs that the Erlkönig has hurt him. The father, shaken in spite of himself, spurs on the horse, and wraps the cloak more warmly around his burden, but when he reaches the town, the child lies dead in his arms.

A single singer represents the narrator and all three characters,—the child, the father, and the Erlkönig, unfolding a dramatic tragedy with a thunderously dramatic piano accompaniment. The listeners' bewilderment when Schubert attempted to play and sing it is not surprising. He was no singer to start with, and his performance singing three voices and playing the complex piano part at the same time can have done his song scant justice. Nevertheless, later in the evening, when he and his friends joined others at the school they had attended as students, they urged Schubert to let them all hear his new song. After he had read it through once, the tenor Holzapfel volunteered to try the voice part, reading it at sight.

Old Dr. Ruzicka, professor of harmony at the school, listened attentively, deliberated a few moments, then set the seal of his approval upon the song, saying, "If Franzl does it, it must be right. His ideas come direct from Heaven."

ALLONS,
ENFANTS DE LA PATRIE

STRASBOURG IN 1792 was a restless city. The French Revolution was in process, and heads sat uneasily on shoulders. Rouget de Lisle, a young French officer garrisoned there, was keenly aware of the ferment. Poet, singer, and musician, he responded like a sensitive string to the vibrating patriotism of the revolutionaries.

He had become a close friend of Dietrich, the mayor of Strasbourg, and often dined at his home. One evening, when food had run very short in that city of paté de foie gras and truffles, the dinner at Dietrich's was woefully meagre. De Lisle drew a bottle of wine from under his cloak. "Let us drink to Liberty and to our country," he cried in the dramatic fashion of his day. "There will soon be a patriotic celebration in Strasbourg. May these last drops inspire De Lisle with one of those hymns which convey to the soul of the people the intoxication from which they proceed." Glasses clinked, faces brightened.

When the young man went home, it was not to sleep. He seated himself at his harpsichord, struck a few chords, hummed, scribbled words.

This went on all night, without his writing a line of music. In the morning, he feverishly set down the words and music of the Marseillaise as they had come to him during the night, and rushed with them to Dietrich's house. Neighbors were hastily collected and brought in to listen. Dietrich's daughter seated herself at the harpsichord and played the accompaniment, while the young man sang. All the listeners were thunderstruck with its rousing phrases. No hit song ever met with a more immediate and enthusiastic response, and it was circulated without delay.

A few months later, poor Dietrich went to the guillotine to the very strains he had heard under such happy circumstances in his own living room. It had become the Frenchman's song of victory and vengeance, his clarion call to action, his hymn of love and hate.

A CLOSE SHAVE FOR
ROSSINI'S *BARBER OF SEVILLE*

THERE WAS A GREAT carnival in Rome in the Fall of 1816. Rossini, then only twenty-four years old, was honored by an invitation to come to the Eternal City, and to pack an opera in his suitcase when he came. He accepted the invitation with alacrity, and in due time presented himself and his score to the impresario of the Teatro Argentina. A recently completed work, *Torwaldoe Dorliska*, was his choice of a carnival opera.

The impresario, much pleased, submitted the libretto to the Chief of Police, with a request for permission to produce it, a bit of red tape that was required even in those pre-Fascist days. But to his chagrin, that gentleman professed to find unseemly political allusions in the text, and no amount of persuasion could shake his decision to forbid its production. What was the unhappy impresario to do? He bethought himself of Beaumarchais' comedy, *The Barber of Seville*, and without consulting the composer, he suggested to the police that Rossini write an opera on that text instead. To this they assented.

When Rossini was informed, he was dismayed. Some years previously, Paisiello, an older composer who was immensely popular in Rome, had written an opera called *The Barber of Seville*, which was still sung and was well known. Rossini felt that it would be presumptuous of him to attempt to rival it, and that Paisiello would be much displeased by his effrontery. But there was no way out. So he wrote to Paisiello, explaining the situation and craving his indulgence, begging his pardon and his permission simultaneously. Both were accorded in a double-edged reply, with the enigmatic statement that Paisiello "had no doubt as to the result."

In thirteen days Rossini had completed the score, and his work was immediately put into rehearsal. The first performance took place on Feb. 5, 1816. Rossini took his place at the harpsichord, his heart thumping so hard that he thought it must surely be heard by the audience. He had every reason to be nervous, for Paisiello had sent a claque to lead the hissing, and they proved to be masters of their trade. They jeered at the tenor, who tuned his guitar on the stage to accompany himself in a solo rendered spiritless by fright and who was duly hissed. They roared because the heroine's entrance aria was presumably not to their liking. They sounded off again when Rossini applauded at the end of Act I to encourage the sorely tried singers. They behaved very badly indeed and Rossini left the theatre before the end of the opera, convinced that it would not be given again.

On sober second-night second thoughts, minus the claque, the audience reconsidered, however. They took note of the sparkling overture, commented on the refreshing absence of long, dry recitativo between the arias. And while deploring the lack of tenderness and passion, they approved the animation and brilliance of the music. Even then, they did not realize that the barber Figaro, flighty, a little vulgar, but very good company, was to become a permanent fixture in opera repertoire.

THE EFFICACY OF A
ROSSINI PRAYER

To ILLUSTRATE the laziness as well as the facility of Rossini, there is a well-worn story to the effect that as he lay in bed one morning, composing, a sheet of manuscript fell off the bed and rolled to the other side of the room. Rather than make the effort involved in getting up to retrieve it, he took another piece of paper, and dashed off another sheet of music, that being the lesser exertion for him.

It seems only fair to match this story with another which also emphasizes his facility. Rossini was lying in bed as usual on the morning after the first performance of his opera, *Moses*, described by Balzac as "a tremendous poem in music." Also as usual, chattering friends occupied every corner of his room. His librettist, Tottola, entered in a state of great excitement. Without stopping to greet anyone, he went straight to the bedside, saying breathlessly, "Maestro, I have rescued the third act."

"What the devil, my friend! From what have you rescued the third act? What have you done?"

"I inserted another prayer for the Hebrews, before they start to cross the Red Sea. Here it is. Look at it. I wrote it in one hour."

"In one hour!" echoed Rossini.

"Yes, I needed no more than one little hour to complete it," boasted Totola.

"Very well. If you have written this in an hour, then I'll set it to music in a quarter of an hour."

He sprang out of bed as quickly as a fat man can spring. He sat down at his table, and in ten minutes, without recourse to the piano or any other instrument, he had composed the prayer which was to become the bright particular hit of the opera.

MEYERBEER'S SLEEPING
BEAUTIES

ROSSINI's *Barber of Seville* was being given in
Paris, at the Opera des Italiens, of which
he was the director. Long before curtain
time, the house was filled to overflowing.
Only two seats remained empty. They happened to be in the front row, where they could
be seen by everybody in the house. People
wondered what great personages they could be
reserved for. Finally, just as the curtain was
about to rise, two elegantly dressed young
men appeared. They conversed together
audibly as they sauntered down the aisle, bowing to right and left, their entrance like a royal
progress. They settled themselves noisily into
the two empty seats, and the curtain rose.
After the first fifteen minutes, their neighbors
heard a gentle snore, followed by another.
They nudged their own neighbors, whispered
"They've fallen asleep. Can you hear them
snore?" The word was passed through the
house. Throughout the opera whose melodies

have delighted the world, the two young men slept serenely. Only at the very end did they arouse themselves, rub their eyes, and stumble out with every evidence of boredom.

Paris buzzed with the incident, and of course Rossini heard about it. He kept his peace, however, until the same thing happened again and yet again, each time at a performance of one of his own operas. Subscribers began to look for the young men to repeat their "act." Then it was whispered about that it really *was* an act. The two young men were engaged by the composer Meyerbeer, whose jealousy of Rossini was notorious, to indicate to him in that way Meyerbeer's opinion of his success.

But Rossini hit back. He sent Meyerbeer two tickets for his opera *Semiramide*, with the following note.

"As I have heard with regret that things have not gone as you wished recently, will you give me the pleasure of accepting these tickets? The box can be seen from every part of the house. The chairs are most comfortable. Shortly before the end of the performance I will have you awakened. In honest admiration,

ROSSINI."

HOW SCHUMANN SAID IT
WITH MUSIC

IN THE 1820's, there lived in a castle in Leipsic
an Ogre named Friedrich Wieck. He had one
beautiful daughter Clara, who was the apple
of his eye,—a bread-winning apple, for at the
age of nine she played the piano so beautifully
that golden ducats were showered upon her
at every performance. Afraid of losing her,
the Ogre kept her most of the time shut up in
her tower practicing, while he gave piano
lessons downstairs. But one day she eluded
her guards, and came into his den just as
Robert Schumann, a composer-prince in the
disguise of a piano pupil, arrived for his lesson. Robert played quite well, but the sounds
he made couldn't compare with those that little
Clara drew from her queer, square-elbowed
instrument. She and her playing cast a powerful spell upon him.

Then one day he came to live in the Ogre's
castle as a pupil. The older he and Clara
grew, the more they were thrown together,

and the more irresistible became the spell
drawing them to each other. Indeed, the
good fairies had endowed her at birth with
such sweetness of character and brilliance of
talent, that she won all hearts. Princes from
many kingdoms sought her out. Robert was
the most constant of them all, but the Ogre
refused pointblank to entertain his suit. The
young man left the castle, the better to compose his mind and his music. But he came
daily to the door of his beloved's abode, only
to be denied admittance. The letters he wrote
her were returned unopened, and her tearful
pleas that she be permitted to see and speak
with him failed to soften the Ogre's stony
heart.

Chuckling maliciously, he whisked her
away to Dresden, and Robert sent her a hurt
little piano piece *Warum*, asking why, though
he knew the answer. Separated for over a
year, the lovers neither saw nor heard from
each other, but Robert composed and dedicated to Clara his *Piano Sonata in F-Sharp Minor*,
a musical love-letter whose meaning she could
not miss. At a concert in Leipzig, she played
his "unique cry of passion" right under her
father's nose, and Robert, tense in the audience, knew that she understood and cared.
He needed that assurance, for Clara, at seventeen, had had a mild flirtation with her sing-

ing teacher, while he himself had so far despaired as to become temporarily engaged to another pianist, Ernestine von Fricken. The *Fantasie* which he composed when he believed that Clara loved another was a wild outpouring, a despairing appeal in the language both understood better than words.

Clara's old nurse and confidante took pity on them, and arranged a moonlight tryst, where the lovers solemnly plighted their troth. On Clara's eighteenth birthday, Robert sent his squire with a scroll, in manly terms asking her father for her hand. Again he was refused; Papa Wieck was a consistent Ogre. But Robert, secure in the knowledge that she loved him, wrote the *Davidsbündlertänze* "amid the most splendid exaltation that I can ever recall" and "with many a bridal thought." During the ensuing months of separation, the *Noveletten*, *Kinderscenen*, and *Kreisleriana* brought Clara repeated musical assurances of his love. She played them at her concerts with the magic only she possessed, and the public began to look upon Robert as a prince of composers, as indeed he was.

Not so Papa Wieck, however. He unleashed all his fury upon the unfortunate young man, invoked the Law, accused him in court of being a drunkard, demanded untold wealth as a marriage settlement. When the Law cleared the accused and sanctioned the marriage, the discomfited Ogre withdrew to sulk in his Castle.

Thus, having performed prodigious feats of valor in music, the prince won his bride. They were married the day before her twenty-first birthday. During that ineffable first year, Robert set over a hundred and thirty poems to music,—the *Myrthen*, *Frauenliebe*, *Dichterliebe* and other great songs. With Clara, he published the *Liebesfrühling—Springtime of Love*—album of songs. He started to work on the *Piano Concerto in A Minor*, which Clara performed triumphantly in Leipsic a couple of years later. And then, as neither voice nor piano could register the surging happiness within him, he turned to the symphony. *Symphony Number One in B-Flat Major* was composed in a month, and in the same year, he completed two others!

Robert and Clara had eight children, and lived happily, though not quite forever after.

THE FADING OF A
FRIENDSHIP

"It is a work of the loftiest kind. I am indeed
proud of the honor you do me in inscribing to
me a composition of such grandeur." In these
words, Franz Liszt graciously acknowledged
the dedication to him by his good friend Robert
Schumann of the *Fantaisie Op. 17*. At that
time, the flame of friendship burned bright
between Schumann, young, poor, and comparatively unknown, and Liszt, already the
idol of music-loving Europe. It had been a
case of love at first sight for them both. After
the first day spent in each other's company,
Liszt averred that it seemed to him that they
must have known each other for twenty years,
and Schumann agreed with him.

Clara Schumann, however, had distinct
reservations. She was cool to the charming
Liszt, and as time went on Robert's enthusiasm
too was tempered. There were artistic dis-
agreements which led to heated discussions.
Inasmuch as Liszt, prolific composer though

he was, took fifteen years before he returned Schumann's compliment by dedicating to him the *Sonata in B Minor*, the Schumanns may have been justified in concluding that fine words butter no dedications.

Still, that does not excuse their rudeness when Liszt called, and offered to play his sonata for them in manuscript before it was published. Schumann took a defensive stand at the piano, and followed the music over Liszt's shoulder as he played. Clara sat listening nearby. At the Adagio, Schumann began to back away until he reached the door, where he stood waiting with obvious impatience for the end. Clara likewise made little attempt to conceal her dislike of the composition, which she later pronounced "horrible." Liszt, man of the world that he was, carried off the situation with his usual flourish, and when the sonata was published, the dedication to Schumann stood.

When the first complimentary copy came to the Schumanns, it arrived at a bad moment. Poor Robert was in an institution, hopelessly insane. Clara had less heart than ever for Liszt and his works and from that time on, she made no secret of her dislike. She refused to attend the unveiling of a monument to Robert after his death, because Liszt was to be there. She extended her dislike even farther.

Irresistible in love, she was implacable in enmity. Thirty years later, when she was editing Schumann's works, she deliberately erased his dedication to Liszt of the Fantaisie in C, Opus 17! The Fantaisie was published without the tribute to Liszt which was to have marked the beginning of a beautiful friendship.

◇◇◇◇◇◇◇◇◇◇◇◇◇◇◇◇◇◇◇◇◇◇◇◇◇◇◇◇

ABBÉ BUT UNCHANGED

AFTER LISZT "got religion" and became an abbé, he adopted the flowing black robe and the air of benignity that went with the title. As he descended his staircase with dignity shortly after the event, he encountered a former pupil who had not seen him in his new role. Taken aback, she greeted him reverently with downcast eyes, and stooped to kiss his hand. But he stooped too, and kissed her cheek. "Let me assure you, my dear," said Abbé Liszt, "that under this austere vestment, the man is still the same."

In truth he was, for not long after this, a young woman tried to commit suicide for love of Abbé Liszt.

CHOPIN'S OWN FUNERAL MARCH

CHOPIN WAS in the dumps. His health was failing; his love affair with George Sand was having more downs than ups; he was morose and dour, quite the man of whom his caustic critic Berlioz said "Il se mourait toute sa vie" (He spent all his life a-dying.) His friends were worried about him, and put their heads together. By way of cheering him, they planned a dinner party in the studio of the artist Ziem. A new piano, to be presented to Chopin as a slight token of their esteem, was installed for the occasion.

The guests were met, the table set, on the appointed day. But where was Chopin? There was no sign of him. Not until long after dinner did he put in an appearance, even more unpunctually than usual. Night had fallen, the studio was dimly lit by candles, but the Prince Polignac, the painter Ricard, and other friends had dined well, and were ready for fun and games, the more absurd the better. After Chopin's arrival, Polignac took a notion to bring out from its closet the skeleton which Ziem sometimes used in painting, and to pose it at the piano. Truly a macabre way of relieving melancholy, but quite in the spirit of the times!

Chopin took no notice of the grotesque figure on the piano bench, but remained alone, off to one side. Polignac crouched in back of the skeleton, waved its arms about, took its hands, and ran the bony fingers over the keys in a weird series of sounds, now loud, now soft. The others kept perfectly still. Suddenly, three hollow raps sounded like a knell. Ricard, to add to the atmospheric pressure, had tapped his foot against the empty chest on which he was sitting.

Everybody laughed except Chopin. He seized the sheet in which the skeleton had been wrapped, draped it over his shoulders, and, as the sound died away, he lunged at the piano stool, seized the skeleton, and embraced it long and ardently. Then, pushing it aside, he seated himself in its place. The others did not realize what had happened, for in the darkness they could barely discern the outlines of the white figure on the stool. Not until they heard the sounds issuing from the piano did they become uneasy. For Chopin was playing as they had never heard him play. It was dead music, music without hope or animation, sounding as if it came from another world. They listened in breathless, terrified silence. Then, in the middle of a measure, the playing broke off suddenly. Chopin had fallen to the floor in a faint. They rushed to pick him up, remorsefully, borne down with self-reproach, and carried him home to his lodgings.

When he gave the first public performance of his B-Flat Minor Sonata some months later, the music he had played at Ziem's gay party appeared in the third movement as a funeral march. And lamentably, the first person to be buried to the sad strains of that music was the composer himself.

A *MIDSUMMER NIGHT'S DREAM* AT MIDDAY

IT WAS A FINE Sunday morning in the summer of 1826. The garden of the Mendelssohn home outside of Berlin buzzed with excitement. On the spreading lawn, under the trees, along the garden walks, chairs had been placed to accommodate the overflow of guests. The friends of the Mendelssohn family had turned out in force to hear Felix's new piece, his *Overture to a Midsummer Night's Dream*.

There was nothing unusual about Sunday morning musicales at the Mendelssohns'; they were a regular event. When the family had moved from the heart of the city to the rambling old house on the outskirts, No. 3 Leipzgerstrasse, "out of the world," they had taken into consideration its many inducements. There was the large music-room in the house itself, besides the Gartenhaus, with its spacious hall opening on to the magnificent lawn and garden. The older Mendelssohns argued that if the music their son Felix had been

writing since his twelfth year was as good as
they thought, their friends should be willing to
make the short trip out from the city to hear
it, especially under such ideal circumstances.
They were right. It was an exceptional Sunday that did not find an expectant audience
assembled in their garden.

Even so, this was a special occasion, and
Felix, his sisters Fanny and Rebekah, and his
brother Paul darted about busily, placing
chairs, greeting guests, seeing that everything
was in order. The *Overture* had been finished
for some time. Felix and his sister Fanny had
played it often in a two-piano version while
he was working on it, and he had polished and
perfected it as well as he could. But this was
to be its first orchestral performance, with
Felix, a handsome boy of seventeen, as conductor. The players were his friends, with a
sprinkling of professionals, all carefully rehearsed by the young composer.

The audience settled down, and to loud
applause Felix took his place on the podium,
the players' eyes fixed adoringly on him. The
introductory notes on the wood-winds ushered
the listeners into an enchanted world, casting
a spell over that first audience, as they have
over all the succeeding ones. For the *Overture*
translated into music all the beauty of Shakespeare's play, beauty of which Felix had an

exquisite awareness. The notes trembled on the air, delicate, elusive, conveying an indescribable charm. The braying of Bottom on the bassoon, a healthy contrast, brought a touch of humor, but the fairy atmosphere clung to the scene. "The guests rubbed their dazzled eyes to make sure that they too were not transported," wrote one of them. "But glancing about them in the garden, with the ancient gloomy yews nodding assent, they were not certain."

MENDELSSOHN AND THE
ST. MATTHEW PASSION

"VERY WELL, then. It is understood. You
give me permission to have the score of Bach's
St. Matthew Passion copied for Felix. I am
very grateful. I will save it as a surprise for
him on his birthday." Mendelssohn's grand-
mother rose with old-world grace, and took
her leave of Zelter, Felix's teacher, the head of
the Berlin Singakademie. Some time later,
the precious score was placed tenderly in
Mendelssohn's eager hands. As Bach's works
were then, in the 1820's, still unplayed, unpublished and unknown, this was a rare gift for
a musician. It marked a milestone in young
Felix's life, for it opened his eyes to new vistas
in the realm of music.

He read and re-read the score until he knew
its every note, could hardly sleep for thinking
of it. He went to Zelter, demanded to know
how it happened that so fine a work had not
been performed in Germany. "Alas! It is
nearly one hundred years since old Father
Bach died," replied Zelter, "and though his

name lives, the majority of those who speak of him as a master are ignorant of the works which made him great."

Felix determined on a Bach crusade. He invited sixteen singers to come to his home once a week, to study and sing the Passion music. In a short time, their enthusiasm matched his own. They began to talk of a possible performance, complete with soloists, double choir, double orchestra, and organ. One of them, Devrient, also a pupil of Zelter's, suggested to Mendelssohn that they ask Zelter to help them put it on at the Singakademie, and talked his friend into going with him to make the proposal.

Nervous but determined, the two young men set out on their errand early in the morning. They found Zelter already seated at his piano, music paper before him, pipe clenched between his teeth. "Well, well, gentlemen," he boomed, "What brings you here so early?" They poured out the story of their rehearsals and their desire to honor the great Bach, concluding with their request. "Impossible!" he replied. "Not to be thought of. Why, it is nothing short of madness. We do not have the facilities here, assuming that we wanted to give the *Passion*. Where would we get all the players, and who would train them if we did get them?" "But it is your fault, Master, that we want to do this. You were the one who taught us to love Bach's music. If it had not been for you, we might never have heard of it." This was a telling point. The old man continued to argue, but his was a losing fight. Finally he had to give in, and before they left, they had his promise to help.

Then Mendelssohn set to work in good earnest. He drilled and rehearsed the performers morning, noon and night, and fired them with his own enthusiasm. He invited professionals and amateurs to the Akademie to listen to the rehearsals and incidentally to become acquainted with the music. By the time the day of the performance (March 11, 1829) arrived, his audience was assured. Every seat was sold, and over a thousand people had been turned away. Mendelssohn conducted; the success of the work was instantaneous.

After the applause had died down, and the lights were extinguished in the hall, Mendelssohn turned to Devrient. "To think that it should have been reserved for an actor, with a Jew," he said quietly, "to restore this great Christian work to the people."

FELIX MENDELSSOHN,
MUSICAL MISSIONARY

WHEN MENDELSSOHN arrived in Munich as a stopping-off place on his cultural tour, in 1831, he was a young man of twenty-two and an optimist. He believed that there he would find a musical life which would be active and inspiring. He wanted to receive, as well as to give musical impetus, and lost no time in visiting all the concert halls, calling on music patrons, and talking with composers and performers. To his disappointment, he found everywhere a strong indifference to serious music. Everybody, it seemed, was afraid of being highbrow, and willing to go to any lengths to avoid so damning an accusation. He was obliged to listen to one insignificant work after another, just as though Haydn, Mozart and Beethoven had never existed. When he protested, he was told that audiences, be they private or public, would tolerate nothing heavier—that in fact they dismissed even the light fare provided for them as being too serious if it didn't happen to appeal to their so-called taste. Mendelssohn bided his time, though quietly determined to do something to change this deplorable state of affairs.

One evening, his opportunity came. He was at a fashionable soirée with music, the music consisting of some showy but trifling piano pieces rattled off by a young lady guest. When she had finished, and while she was acknowledging the applause, Mendelssohn walked over to the piano, and seated himself on the stool she had just vacated. Silently, he addressed his audience, "Well, if you get bored, it serves you right," and launched into the C sharp Minor Sonata of Beethoven, the Moonlight Sonata. It is a long work. He played steadily, with only a slight pause between the movements. When he had finished, he hardly dared turn around to see the effect on his audience. He need not have feared. Some of the ladies were sobbing, others were pale and stunned, while many burst into spontaneous applause. Within a few minutes, the noise in the room was deafening. The men were loudly discussing the importance of the work they had heard. The ladies were crowding around the piano, imploring Mendelssohn to play more, handing him paper and pencil so that he could write for them the names of other Beethoven sonatas which they might learn to play, begging him to teach them.

His experiment was even more of a success than at first appeared. The next morning, the Countess in whose house the musicale had been held asked him to order good editions of Mozart, Beethoven, and Weber for her library. When the musicians of Munich heard this bit of news, which traveled fast, they took the hint and followed suit. So did the patrons of the arts, the composers, the concert artists. And Mendelssohn was able to resume his travels with a light heart. The quality of the programs in Munich showed a marked improvement after his visit.

A DOUBLE SURPRISE

FREDERIC CHOPIN had moved from his old lodgings to new rooms in Paris. This was an event in his friends' lives as well as his own, for he was as hospitable as he was gifted. Naturally, they were eager to see his new rooms, and awaited, as their right, an invitation to a house-warming party. But none was forthcoming. The poets Heine and Mickilewicz, the singer Adolphe Nourrit, the composers Meyerbeer and Liszt, Delacroix the painter, the novelist Georges Sand, and the beautiful Comtesse d'Agoult, who wrote novels under the pseudonym of Daniel Stern, expected a party and were determined to have one. But Chopin was in no hurry. He kept saying that he didn't have all his furniture, that he couldn't fix a date, that he was too busy—in other words that he couldn't be bothered.

At last, the group took matters into their own hands. They arranged among themselves, unknown to Chopin, to meet at the new rooms on an evening in 1833, bringing their own supper. At the appointed hour of midnight, they arrived in high spirits, each

with a bulging brown paper bag under his
arm. Chopin could do no less than invite
them in, light the candles, and show them
around. Soon he was the gayest of them all.
After the good French sausage and crusty
bread, washed down with wine, little urging
was required to make him sit down at the
piano and play. To two of the gathering,
his music that night seemed to carry a special
message.

Young Franz Liszt, even as he marveled at
the delicacy of Chopin's piano arabesques,
marveled equally at the beauty of Mme.
d'Agoult, whose face was reflected in a mirror
facing him. He could not take his eyes from
her image. He was blond, handsome, twenty-
two. She was twenty-eight, in the full bloom
of youth, her freshness enhanced by contrast
with her husband the count, older than she
by twenty years. She appeared cold and dis-
tant. In fact, she was described by a contemporary as "six feet of ice on top of twenty
feet of lava." The ice melted that evening in
the warmth of Liszt's ardent glances, and when
he asked permission to call, it was granted.
Their friendship ripened fast, the more so as
the susceptible Liszt was on the rebound from
a disappointment in love.

Theirs is a charming love-story, a meeting
of minds and hearts. He visited her daily, was
close beside her when her child, Louison, died,
became in fact, if not in name, her husband.
Later, she left the Comte d'Agoult to throw
in her lot with Liszt's. They had three children, and she made a home for him, to which
he returned from long, exhausting tours, to
find rest and solace. Their relation, during the
ten years it endured, was idyllic. For them,
Chopin's innocent little surprise party marked
a bigger surprise, a turning point in both their
lives.

WEBER'S *EURYANTHE*

"MAKE ROOM FOR ME! I am the poetess!" A harsh voice rose insistently above the tumult of the first night audience in the Kärntnerthor Court Opera Theater in Vienna. The voice belonged to a stout, sloppy female with a long shawl drooping from her shoulders, who was pushing her way from seat to seat, peering near-sightedly at the numbers. She proclaimed loudly that she had forgotten her ticket, and not until a burst of applause marked the appearance of the composer, Carl Maria von Weber, did she subside into a seat. It was the opening night of Weber's opera *Euryanthe.* Ticket or none, she did not intend to forego the pleasure of hearing it, not only because his first opera, *Der Freischutz,* had been so successful, but also because she had a personal stake in *Euryanthe.* She had written the libretto.

True, the sloppy lady, whose name was Helmine von Chézy, had been obliged by Weber to revise her text to *Euryanthe* no less than nine times. True, he was by no means satisfied with it despite all the revisions, but had resigned himself to its imperfections rather than start again with a different librettist. Since Mme. von Chézy had previously written a libretto to Schubert's *Rosamunde*, Weber tried to believe that her *Euryanthe* text was not as bad as he knew it to be. (It was recently described as "a libretto that reads like a hoax by Robert Benchley.")

The first performance took place on Oct. 25, 1823. The next day, the composer wrote to his wife. "My reception, when I appeared in the orchestra, was the most enthusiastic and brilliant one could imagine. There was no end to it. At last I gave the signal for the beginning. Stillness of death. The overture was applauded madly; there was a demand for a repetition; but I went ahead, so that the performance might not be too long drawn out."

Thus neither the eccentric Mme. von Chézy nor her bad libretto prevented Weber's beautiful music from pleading the cause of German opera so eloquently, that first night in Vienna and in many other places afterward, that it set a new fashion in music-drama.

HOW THE CELLO
ACQUIRED ITS PEG

FAT STOMACHS are responsible for a number of musical improvements. Witness the crossing of hands on the piano keyboard, an expedient adopted by Domenico Scarlatti when his bulk prevented his getting close enough to the harpsichord to execute the rapid passages he had written. Witness, too, the elevation of the cello from a position tightly clutched between the player's knees to the dignity and stability of a peg planted firmly on the floor.

The cello's uplift came about in this way. François Servais, a renowned Belgian cellist who lived from 1807 to 1866, in his youth played the cello as everyone else did, held off the floor by the grip of his knees. His short legs were a handicap—but since he was slim and young and gifted, he was able to overcome that handicap satisfactorily. As he grew older, however, the good food of Brussels took effect on his physique, and he developed an enormous abdomen which, with his short legs and small stature, transformed him into a truly tubby little man. It became immensely difficult for him to open his legs wide enough, and grip the instrument firmly enough, to play at all, much less to play well. He was something of a mechanic as well as musician, and when he realized what was happening to his performing ability, he took action. He had a peg made, to be inserted into a fixture he devised at the base of the cello. The peg could be raised or lowered, according to the player's physical conformation. He tried his invention in private, and found it good. He tried it in public, and his audiences made no objection. Other musicians commented and criticized, but on the whole they approved. Thenceforth, he used a peg, and taught his pupils to do so.

One of these pupils, Jules Delsart, later became a teacher of cello at the Brussels Conservatory. He was delighted with Servais' ingenious contraption, and himself always used a peg. Yet, at the same time, he considered the concession to comfort something of an unmanly weakness. Perhaps he feared that the fashion might change, and that peg-users would in time come to be ridiculed as softies. At any rate, when he had his portrait painted to hang in the Conservatory, he undressed his cello to the extent of omitting the peg and having it omitted from the picture.

The cellists in the Opera House in Brussels, on the other hand, had no such scruples, nor did they concern themselves with appearances. They had found it no pleasure to sit for hours cramped in the orchestra pit, with their cellos held tightly between their knees, awaiting the cue for an occasional oom-pah-pah. In fact, they had gotten in the habit of cheating. They rested their instruments directly on the floor and played them so, trusting to luck that, though the tone was muffled and of inferior quality, it would not be noticed, since theirs

was a subordinate voice. They enthusiastically followed Servais' lead, and fitted their cellos with the saving pegs. Nor did they make any secret of what they had done. As time went on, more and more cellists adopted the peg as a permanent fixture. Today it is in general use, and most people have doubtless forgotten that it was not always there.

FAIR EXCHANGE

THE OLDER Johann Strauss, Waltz King the First, sat at his piano one day while his little boy Johann played about the room. A new waltz was in process of creation, and Strauss was trying various combinations on the piano.

As most composers do at some point, he got stuck. He wanted to find an interesting modulation from one key to another, but none of the chords he tried satisfied him. As he muttered anathemas under his breath, the little boy wandered over and stood beside him. He placed his hands on the piano, and using the theme of the waltz, he played a pleasant, spontaneous modulation. "Couldn't you do it like this?" he inquired innocently.

His father was not over-pleased. Already he was discouraging the boy's musical inclinations, fearful of the competition which the future might—and did—bring. "I'll tell you what," he rumbled. "In future, you may compose my waltzes, and I'll do your school work."

THE WALTZ KING IS DEAD,
LONG LIVE THE
WALTZ KING

THE TIME is October, 1844, the place Vienna.
The Dommayer Casino, where fashionable
Viennese imbibe their coffee and whipped
cream, presents to the world a wall placarded
with announcements. Around one placard
in particular successive groups linger, ex-
citedly discussing its contents. With many
exclamation points, it invites all and sundry
to a Soirée Dansante, featuring the first appearance in the café of Johann Strauss Junior,
conducting his own orchestra.

Behind that billboard lies a story. For
years, Johann's father has been the acknowledged waltz king of Vienna. At court, in
cafés, in the streets, people have danced to the
lilting waltzes composed and directed by
him. He has no intention of allowing a young
whippersnapper, son or no son, to dispute his
title, and has bestirred himself accordingly.
He has summoned his devoted friend Hirsch.

"This must be stopped, and at once," he commands. Hirsch obediently sets out to visit all the fashionable restaurants, threatening them with loss of the popular conductor's services if they employ the son. Hirsch wears out shoe-leather with good results, until he comes to Dommayer, proprietor of a suburban but heavily patronized café in Hietzing. Dommayer shrewdly senses the publicity value in a situation which pits son against father. He engages young Johann, plasters Vienna with advance publicity, plays up the début into an important event.

When the evening arrives, Dommayer's café is crowded to the doors, every table is occupied to the tune of thirty to fifty kronen a ticket, and a huge overflow audience is turned away. In an inconspicuous corner sits Hirsch, with Haslinger, sent by the dog-in-the-manger father to report happenings, and to hiss the upstart off the stage. Young Johann leaps to the platform, violin and bow held gracefully in one hand. Applause rocks the house before a note is sounded. Using the bow as baton, he conducts the orchestra in Auber's melodious overture to *La Muette de Portici*. He follows this with a waltz of his own, which he plays on the violin, facing the audience in the Strauss tradition. None can resist the handsome young man whose playing is equally

handsome. From that moment, he holds the
audience in the hollow of his baton. They demand three repetitions of that waltz, and as
others follow, they clamor for more and more,
bringing the number of encores as high as

nineteen for a single piece. At the conclusion
of the program, young Johann, with a fine
sense of showmanship, plays his father's
Lorelei-Rheinklänge (Rhine songs of the

Lorelei). This is the straw that breaks the back of the opposition. While the sentimental Viennese cheer to the echo, Hirsch and Haslinger make their way to the platform. They hoist young Johann on their shoulders, and carry him, thus enthroned, around the Casino. By that act, they crown him king. For the time being, Johann Senior is forgotten. Later all is forgiven, and he and his son play joint concerts—friends once more.

MY COUNTRY, 'TIS
OF THEE

DR. LOWELL MASON was running out of tunes
for his Sunday-school classes. And no wonder!
It had been his idea in the first place to teach
singing to the children in Boston's schools and
Sunday schools. As his reward—or punishment—he was obliged not only to teach, but
also to keep them supplied with material.
And that meant that he was constantly on the
lookout for good tunes, and was kept busy
himself composing hymn-tunes for them.

His friend, William Woodbridge, who was
traveling abroad, knew of his difficulties, and
when returning from a trip brought him a
book of songs from Germany. Dr. Mason was
delighted, but as he knew no German, he was
unable to translate the words. So he asked
Samuel Francis Smith, a young student at
Andover, to look through the book and translate anything that appeared to him to be
worthwhile.

Accordingly, one rainy afternoon Smith
dutifully picked up the book, hummed through

a few of the tunes, perhaps recognized the tune of *God Save the King*, and liked it. He wrote a set of patriotic words to fit it, beginning "My Country, 'Tis of Thee"—which probably had nothing to do with the words already there. Then he shoved the book and paper into his desk drawer, and dismissed the whole business from his mind. Eventually, however, he got around to sending his verses to Lowell Mason, who promptly made use of them. He taught them to all his classes.

The song made its début at a big Sunday-school festival at the Park Street Church in Boston on the Fourth of July, 1832. All Mason's child singers were there, and they sang with a gusto that sped the song to fame. It rapidly became, though not actually the national anthem, one of the best loved and most sung of all the American patriotic songs.

GO, MY THOUGHT,
ON GOLDEN WINGS

ONE SNOWY EVENING in 1841, young Giuseppe Verdi ploughed wearily through the streets of Milan, his head sunk between his shoulders, a prey to the deepest melancholy. Tears fell unheeded as he thought back to the time, only a few short months before, when he had been blissfully happy. His adored wife Margherita and their two small children had been all the world to him. He had had his work too, assured by contract with the impresario Merelli, which stipulated that he was to deliver three operas for immediate production. Life was sweet. Then sudden death had struck down first the little boy, then the girl, and finally Margherita. At one blow he had lost all he loved. Stricken to the heart, he had taken to his bed. He had sold everything, even pawned Margherita's jewels to pay the rent. And all the while he was under contract to compose music for—of all things—a comic opera! He completed it, called it *Un Giorno di Regno* (King for a Day), and it had run for just about that long, so coolly had it been received by public and critics. Its failure had filled Verdi's cup of bitterness to overflowing. As he walked, he thought for the hundredth time, "If only the public had, I do not say *applauded*, but received the opera in silence, I could not have found words to thank them." But the audience, perhaps unaware of the circumstances under which the opera had been composed, had hooted and jeered. Those sounds rang in his ears now as he paced sadly through the snow.

Some-one touched his arm. "It's Merelli," a voice murmured in his ear. "Ah, Merelli," he echoed dully.

"Yes, it's Merelli. How are you, my boy? It's a long time since I've seen you. What are you doing?"

"Nothing. Nothing much. I went to Busseto for awhile to visit Margherita's father. It was torture. I couldn't stand it. I came back to Milan to teach. I have a few pupils. I am not writing anything. You destroyed my contract of course, as I asked you to?"

"Of course, of course. But still, I'm interested in anything you care to write."

"But I don't care to write. I told you that. I only read. I read anything and everything, mostly stories and novels. Only to forget!"

"Very well, my friend, just as you wish."

They walked together for a time in silence. Then Merelli said "I too have my disappointments. Your old pal Solera wrote a fine libretto for an opera about Nebuchadnezzar. I engaged Nicola to write the music. And now Nicola has refused to do the music. Says he doesn't like the libretto."

"Too bad," indifferently rejoined Verdi. "Why not substitute another opera then, perhaps *Il Proscritto?*"

"That's an idea. Walk to the theatre with me, will you?"

Verdi morosely assented. While Merelli left him to hunt for the desired work in the theatre library, he cunningly gave Verdi Solera's libretto, saying "Just look it over, if you don't mind." "I don't want to read any libretto." "O come on, read it. It can't do you any harm." Grudgingly, Verdi stuck it in his pocket. When he arrived at his home, he threw it on the table. It fell open, and his eye lighted on the line "Va, pensiero, sull ali dorati" (Go, my thought, on golden wings). Drawn to it in spite of himself, he read a little more, then angrily pushed it away and went to bed. To bed, but not to sleep. The line drew him irresistibly. At last, he rose and lit his candle. Before morning, he had read the libretto through three times, and had committed most of it to memory.

The next day, he went to Merelli to return it. "Sit down, sit down," urged the impresario cordially. "Well, what did you think of the libretto?"

"It's very fine," replied Verdi.

"Then set it to music."

"Not a chance."

"Set it to music, I tell you. Set it to music."

Merelli laughingly stuffed the manuscript into the young man's pocket, pushed him out of the room, and locked the door on him.

Verdi went home. There was nothing else to do. He tried to dismiss the libretto but it refused to be dismissed. Gradually, like sensation returning to a numbed limb, musical ideas began to take shape in his mind. At last he succumbed to their insistence, and within three months, he completed the opera *Nabuco* (Nebuchadnezzar). He took it to Merelli, who was dumbfounded at the speedy completion of the task. Verdi demanded that he fulfil his promise to produce the opera. He demanded, furthermore, that it be given at Carnival time, the most favorable moment for new works. Merelli cautiously advised delay, inasmuch as he had already contracted for three new operas by well-known composers, but Verdi insisted. He raged, stormed, wept and cajoled, even wrote Merelli a most insulting letter. Finally, the impresario had to agree to produce *Nabuco* during Carnival week, provided Verdi would permit him to use stock costumes and scenery, since there was no time to design and prepare new ones. "Naturalmente" (Of course) replied the composer.

The story has a happy ending. The opera, produced with the finest singers, was a complete success. The public went mad. The roar of approval at the end of the first act was so overwhelming that Verdi, seated, as was the custom, in the orchestra pit, was terrified and believed his opera lost. Later, reassured, he took a bow and accepted the tributes showered upon him. *Nabuco*, so inauspiciously begun, proved the foundation of his later fame.

THE EVER-POPULAR
IL TROVATORE

VERDI WAS SEATED at his desk, at work on his new opera one day, when a visitor was announced. A well-known music critic was ushered in, and Verdi greeted him cordially. "Just the man I want to see," he said as he shook hands. "If you can stand it, I'd like to try a few bits from *Il Trovatore*, the opera I'm just finishing, and see how you like them. Would you mind?" "I'd be delighted," replied the visitor, and seated himself expectantly in a comfortable chair.

The composer plunged into the *Anvil Chorus*, and then, with a sidewise glance at his one-man audience, went on to the aria *Fierce Flames Are Soaring*, following it with the *Soldier's Chorus* and the *Miserere*, tunes now known to all. He played them with spirit, singing as he played. At the end, he turned on his stool, said "Well?" The critic's expression was pained. He shook his head. "Frankly," he said, "it's no good. That *Anvil Chorus* is trash, the rest of it is no better. Pure rubbish! This time, Maestro, you have failed."

"My dear friend, I am delighted," beamed Verdi. "I have been composing a popular opera, in which I was resolved to please everybody except great critics and classicists like you. Had I pleased them, I'd have pleased no-one else. What you say assures my opera of success. I am most grateful." He bowed out his visitor. Within a few months, *Il Trovatore* had become a favorite of opera lovers all over the world.

THE LAST HOPE

IT IS ALWAYS edifying to think of a composer as a human being. So the story that Louis Moreau Gottschalk, American pianist-composer, first played his tremulous piano piece, *The Last Hope*, at the bedside of the dying friend for whom he had composed it, has for many years drawn tears and words of praise from his sentimental admirers.

An amusing corollary to this story appeared when Gottschalk first had his tear-jerker published. He went to the printer's office to pick up the proofs, and as he came out, met his friend, the pianist William Mason. "Read that!" he commanded, flourishing the title-page. William read and laughed. *The Last Hope* had emerged from the press as *The Latest Hops*.

LAND OF COTTON

IT WAS A COLD, rainy day in 1859. Daniel Emmett's Minstrel Troupe were rehearsing in an unheated theatre in New York. They were miserably conscious of the snow falling out-doors, and the mercury falling in the ther-mometer. They were tired to death of the long, cold winter, and longing for a warmer spot. "When are we going South, Dan?" was the question on everyone's lips. Dan could only shake his head. "I know it's cold here, boys. I don't like it any better than you do. But we're playing to sold-out houses and the money is rolling in. We can't quit now if you want your salaries paid. We'll have to stick it awhile longer. "Ah, I wish I was in Dixie," muttered the end man.

On a blue Monday morning several days later, Emmett stood at the window of his room, twirling the shade-cord, and looking morosely at the driving rain. His wife was doing the family washing, and to the accompaniment of splashing suds, she was scolding Emmett, in wifely fashion, for something he had done or left undone. "Ah, I wish I was in Dixie," he muttered savagely. Mrs. Emmett stopped both washing and scolding. "Why, Dan," she exclaimed, "that's a good line for the new song you have to write."

Emmett's face cleared. He began to hum a tune, *Dixie*. It was the hit of his show. Later it became the preferred marching song of the Confederate army. When peace came, *Dixie* was sung by North and South alike, in a new spirit of brotherhood.

BERLIOZ' UNWRITTEN SYMPHONY

HECTOR BERLIOZ lay in bed, wide awake, staring into the darkness. The clock struck midnight. Close beside him he was aware of the uneasy breathing of his invalid wife, Henrietta, and an occasional moan of pain. The baby, Louis, stirred restlessly in his crib. The clock ticked away the seconds of another sleepless night.

His mind reverted to the past. He saw himself, an ardent red-haired youth, starving in Paris, but nevertheless paying violent court to the woman who now lay beside him. She had been ice to his flame. She had driven him to the most absurd pretexts for seeing her; he recalled the time he had thrown himself at her feet in the street, threatening suicide if she refused to receive him. Although she was an actress, she still could not distinguish between play-acting and the real thing, and she had dismissed him and his passion, sincere as they were, as utterly mad. He smiled bitterly in the darkness at the recollection of the pain of that dismissal, and of her departure for England without a word of hope or farewell.

He had revenged himself by writing a symphony! For weeks, he had barely eaten or slept, had not known there was anything in the world except his work. When the *Symphonie Fantastique* was finished, he had dedicated it to Henrietta. He had put her into every frenzied phrase, and had written a program to the music, in which he pilloried her for her wanton indifference to his suffering. And then the miracle had happened.

A reminiscent happiness suffused him as he thought of the evening when, sitting at his kettle-drums in the orchestra, tuning up for a performance of the symphony, he saw her in a box. Accident had brought her there; he thought it was fate. Regardless of the audience, he had expressed his passion in unrestrained gestures and grimaces as the symphony proceeded. Every thump on the drums was addressed to her. Henrietta had been flattered and pleased, rather than embarrassed. She had smiled, and had consented to meet him afterward. He had seen her a few times after that, and now here they were, man and wife.

He tossed restlessly. The *Fantastic Symphony* was all very well. It had been praised, and had brought him some recognition. But he ought to write another. He really wanted to;

his was a genuine urge. And on the heels of the thought, a theme flashed through his mind.

This was the inspiration he had been waiting for. Rapidly, the opening measures took shape—he had it! He decided to set it right down on paper, that was the only way. He would go quietly, quietly, down to his desk. Carefully, he raised himself on his elbow. Henrietta stirred, the baby whimpered. He waited. She called fretfully, "Hector, are you there?" He sank back. "And if I succeed in writing the score of a symphony, then what?" he asked himself. "It will take months and months of time that I cannot spare. It will cost at least a thousand francs to have the parts copied. Then I will have to arrange for its publication, its performance. What about the musical criticisms I've been writing? How can we get along without the money those bring in? Alas! For doctors and nurses alone I spent hundreds of francs last month. The baby's milk, the delicacies for Henrietta, have to be paid for. A symphony now is an extravagance I cannot afford. . . . But I must write it, I must."

For hours, he argued with himself, his desire to put pen to paper as powerful as that of a drinker for his glass. But still he remained where he was. The next night and the next, he wrestled with temptation. He wrote to a close friend, describing his struggle to dismiss the swarming musical ideas. Then he was rewarded, if reward it was. The inspiration left him as suddenly as it had come. He lost the theme that had so attracted him, and could not have written the symphony if he would. And the world was the poorer by a symphony from the pen of one of the greater composers for orchestra that ever lived.

GLINKA'S "BOOST"

"THERE'S NO pleasing some people," complained Mme. Schestakoff, sister of the Russian nationalist composer, Glinka, to a friend. "I'd like to cheer up my brother, he is so depressed. But I don't know what to do. I'm so afraid of doing the wrong thing."

"What does he like?"

"He'd listen to Beethoven all day and all night. He cried when he heard *Fidelio*—I was with him. And after the Symphony in A, the Seventh, he came home to my sister-in-law so overcome he couldn't talk to her for hours."

"It hardly seems to have a cheering effect on him."

"No, I believe he compares his own compositions with Beethoven's and finds them mediocre. You know, when his opera *Ruslan and Ludmilla* was given in 1840, the St. Petersburg high and mighties said it was 'music for coachmen.' And my brother retorted, 'What's the difference, since the coachmen are obviously superior to their masters?' But it hurt him, nevertheless, and I believe that Beethoven's music makes him feel that perhaps those aristocrats were not so far wrong about him."

"You'll have to do something. He's a great man, and he needs a boost."

"I have an idea. I see in the newspaper that his opera *The Life of the Tsar* is to be given this week. I'll invite him to go to the theatre with me, and I'll not tell him what we are going to hear. I believe he'll be agreeably surprised."

Accordingly, an evening in 1856 found Glinka and his sister seated together in a box at the opera. Glinka had not witnessed a performance of *The Life of the Tsar* in the twenty years since it was first given. Apparently, nothing had been done to the original properties in all those twenty years! He recognized the costumes, grown old and worn, the stage sets, dusty and outmoded. The singers and orchestra gave a second-rate performance. The opera had been buried alive. If a scheduled work could not be given, *The Life of the Tsar* was exhumed.

Glinka sat through the evening in a state of acute misery. The sense of neglect overwhelmed him. He was recognized and a few loyal admirers made an abortive attempt to arrange an ovation for him at the end of the performance. When he learned of their intention, he left the opera house hurriedly by a side entrance, before the final curtain. A severe nervous attack was the result of Mme. Schestakoff's well-meant effort to cheer him.

BORIS GODOUNOFF,
HAND-TAILORED OPERA

MOUSSORGSKY'S *Boris Godounoff* was a savagely anti-fascist opera, though at the time it was produced (1874) the word fascism was unknown. It uttered powerful tonal blasts against tyranny and totalitarianism; its crashing chords called for justice for the downtrodden masses, mercy for the poverty-stricken, punishment for evil-doers. No wonder it was withdrawn after a few performances; Czarist Russia had no stomach for such plain speaking, even when disguised behind a Pushkin story and cloaked in magnificent music.

When Moussorgsky died, in 1881, the manuscript of the opera lay upon his shelves. It had been performed, then forgotten. Its rugged beauty amazed and humbled the friends and musical executors with whom he had constituted "the Five" of Russian music. Balakireff, Cui, Rimsky-Korsakoff and Borodin decided that *Boris* must be given to the public, and Rimsky-Korsakoff undertook to revise the manuscript.

He was a master of orchestration, but his style of writing was as different from Moussorgsky's as he was himself. He was polished, suave, and aristocratic in his writing, as in his person. He undoubtedly did his best to preserve the original as closely as possible. But he could not help smoothing out the Moussorgskyan bumps and angles into a more decorous pattern. And although the opera has had a terrific impact whenever his version was performed, there have been many who have felt that it has lost all too much Moussorgsky by Rimsky-Korsakoff's revision.

So strong was that feeling in young Dmitri Shostakovitch, the present-day Soviet composer, that in 1944 he brought out his own version of the music. It has been said that Shostakovitch "writes for the masses with a sense of grim reality," and by that token he should be the heir to Moussorgsky's spirit. Yet, save for a slightly coarser musical texture, he made surprisingly few changes in the Rimsky-Korsakoff version. To the casual listener, his *Boris* sounds much as it has always sounded. It appears that *Boris* will continue to be tailored until some enterprising impresario returns to the original model and puts on the opera as it was written by Moussorgsky.

A PETITION

AT ONE OF THE early performances of *Boris Godounoff*, it was decided that the chorus should present a petition to the Czar for the redress of a grievance. At the close of one of the scenes of the opera, the curtain was to be rung up, and the chorus revealed, kneeling in supplication, all eyes turned toward the imperial box. A representative of the chorus was then to hand the petition to His Imperial Highness.

Chaliapin, who was singing *Boris*, was not informed of the plan. When the curtain rose, he was still in his place on the stage, attired in the royal robes of his role. Czar Boris of the opera confronted Czar Nicholas II for one long, tense moment. Then, joining the crowd in supplication, Chaliapin bent his own knee. The Czar was pleased to smile graciously and grant the plea, and Chaliapin became even more popular, as the people's champion, than he had been as their preferred singer.

ALEXANDER BORODIN,
M.D., D.M.

ALEXANDER BORODIN, M.D., was a modest man.
Music was his true love, chemistry his pro-
fession. And so he allowed his gifts as a sci-
entist to be emphasized, his music to be under-
rated. Tchaikowsky and others looked down
their noses at him as an amateur in music because of this dual loyalty. Yet his claim to
immortality is based, not on his juggling of
germs, but on his superb opera *Prince Igor*, and
his symphonies, written under difficulties that
would have defeated a lesser genius.

For example, the première of his Second
Symphony climaxed a series of accidents that
read like a nightmare. He himself described
them in a letter to an intimate friend.

"The Musical Society had determined to
perform my Second Symphony at one of its
concerts. I was in the country, and did not
know this fact. When I came back to St.
Petersburg, I could not find the first movement
and the finale. The score of these movements
was lost; I had without doubt mislaid it. I

hunted everywhere, but could not find it; yet the Society insisted, and there was hardly time to have the parts copied. What should I do? To crown all, I fell sick. I could not shuffle the thing off, and I was obliged to re-orchestrate my symphony. Nailed to my bed by fever, I wrote the score in pencil. My copy was not ready in time, and my symphony will not be performed till the next concert. My two symphonies then will be performed in the same week. Never has a professor of the Academy of Medicine and Surgery been found in such a box!"

He called himself in this letter, not a composer, but a "professor of the Academy of Medicine!" But elsewhere he described himself as "always a poet in my soul," and it is as such that he escaped from his "box" to immortalize Russian knighthood in his music.

THE "PERFECT OPERA" AND ITS IMPERFECT CRITICS

WHEN GEORGES BIZET selected as a suitable subject for an opera a novel that had sold many thousands, he displayed the same business sense as movie producers when they film a *Gone with the Wind* or *For Whom the Bell Tolls*. The Carmen of Prosper Merimée's yellow paper-backed novel, bad girl though she was, had wheedled her wicked way into the hearts of all Paris before he decided to set her exploits to music. He had no thought of immortalizing her; she was material that presented itself so that he might do a job that was expected of him, as a composer. He did not know, as he set down the music which later became familiar to all music lovers, that he was writing what in time came to be known as the perfect opera.

The first performance was given on March 3, 1875. Bizet attended it, a nervous bundle of hopes and fears, as the curtain arose. Alas! It was the fears which were realized. Despite

the hard work that had gone into the writing
and rehearsing, the performance was afterward described as "a deadly frost! An audience like ice! Not a single effect; nothing
made a hit!" In other words, a flop. Deeply
depressed, Bizet went home before the third
act. It was well that he did, for he needed a
night's sleep to fortify himself for the next day.

With rare unanimity, the newspaper critics
fell upon the opera and tore it, shapely limb
from limb. They had not a good word to say
for it. As to the libretto, one wrote "The love
of two such odious creatures as Carmen and
Don José could hardly inspire a musician like
Bizet"; another "This Carmen, who would be
too bold and free at the Elysées-Montmartre
or at Valentino, is a subject for the solicitude of
physicians rather than one to interest respect-
able spectators going to the Opéra Comique
with their wives and daughters." This in
Paris, where "l'amour" has always been on an
equal footing with "liberté, égalité, and fra-
ternité!"

As to the music, it was condemned as being
—of all things—Wagnerian. That seems an
odd description of the warm, melodious songs
and the full yet balanced orchestral accompaniment of Carmen, which lent themselves to a
popularized version in Carmen Jones as no
Wagnerian opera could. One critic declared

that only three pieces in the music had an ending and were therefore effective, another that "In the brushwood of the score there was now and then a fragment of an accessible phrase, but the orchestra was constantly babbling and saying things that were not demanded of it."

Bizet was crushed under the weight of disapproval. He began to believe that the critics must be right. The applause of the audience at subsequent successful performances did not alter the tenor of the press comment, nor renew his belief in his work. Although the opera was a brilliant triumph when performed in Vienna in the Fall, Bizet was not there to see it. He had died the preceding June, three months after the Paris première.

A SNAP JUDGMENT

In 1874, Tchaikowsky wrote, in a letter to his soul-mate, Mme. von Meck, "I am wallowing in the composition of a piano concerto with my whole soul. It is going very badly." This was the B flat Minor Piano Concerto, always well known to serious musicians, and latterly to lovers of popular music as well, thanks to the syncopated arrangement played by dance bands.

Engrossed as he was in his duties as teacher at the Conservatory in Moscow, Tchaikowsky had little time for composition. But he completed his concerto by keeping everlastingly at it. And he could hardly wait to show it to Nikolai Rubinstein, his superior in the Conservatory, to whom he had dedicated it. Barely was the ink dry before he invited Rubinstein and another colleague, Hubert, to meet him in one of the Conservatory classrooms for a private hearing. On Jan. 5, 1875, on his way to a party, Tchaikowsky met them there, greeted them cordially, placed his manuscript on the music rack of the piano,

and began to play. In a letter written in all
bitterness a few days later, he described their
reception of his efforts.

"I played the first movement. Not a word,
not one remark. Have you ever had the
awkward and absurd experience of cooking
and serving good food to a friend only to have
him remain silent? . . . I did not want
aesthetic criticism of my composition, but
only technical comment. Rubinstein's silence
was thunderous . . . I found strength to play
the concerto right through. More silence!
'Well?' I inquired as I got up from the piano.
Then a stream poured from Rubinstein's
mouth. My concerto was valueless, wholly
unperformable. The passage work was so
fragmentary, disconnected, and poorly composed, that it could not be ameliorated. The
composition itself was bad, trivial, vulgar.
Here and there I had filched from others.
Perhaps one or two pages were worth saving;
the rest must be destroyed, or completely re-
composed. And so on, and so on . . . The
chief element I cannot reproduce, the tone of
voice in which all this was uttered."

Hubert timidly echoed Rubinstein's dictum,
in a kindlier tone, but with unmistakable disapproval. Struck down by their reaction,
Tchaikowsky left the room without a word, and
repaired to an empty classroom to conceal his

agitation. He was close to tears. A few minutes later, Rubinstein entered. "On second thoughts," he said, "if you will revise the concerto as I indicated, I will perform it at my concert." "Over my dead body," retorted Tchaikowsky. "I shall not alter one single note. I shall publish the work exactly as it is." And so he did. Furthermore, he erased the name of Rubinstein from the dedication, and inserted in its place that of von Bülow, who promised to perform it just as it was written. In acknowledging the gift copy sent to him, von Bülow wrote "I am proud to have been honored by the dedication of this splendid work of art, ravishing in all its aspects."

Thus Tchaikowsky's concerto was saved, but the wound inflicted by Rubinstein's churlishness was never completely healed.

FROM BODY TO SOUL

"Say, brothers, will you meet us on Canaan's happy shore?"

To THE TUNE of John Brown's body, these words were sung by two homesick Southern boys in the Tiger regiment one lazy Sunday afternoon. An equally homesick captain, passing through, heard the men, and went off humming the tune to himself. It stuck. When Pat Gilmore brought his band to play for the regiment, the captain passed the tune on to him, he played it, and the men joined in with all their throats.

But they didn't much care for the words, and tried parodying them. There was a big clumsy Scotchman in the regiment named John Brown, whom they loved to tease. He was no relative to John Brown of Ossawatomie, but the similarity of names made the words "John Brown's body lies a 'mouldering in the grave" a particularly unpleasant form of teasing. So they used them for a new marching song, with many stanzas, some not printable. And it percolated to other Southern regiments in the Civil War.

One day, Julia Ward Howe, the poetess, made an excursion from Washington to the battlefield outside the city limits. The men rode into the fight singing their song. She was enchanted with the tune, but not with the words. And that evening, she wrote the stirring poem beginning "Mine eyes have seen the glory of the coming of the Lord." Both sets of words are popular today.

OLD FOLKS AT HOME

"COME ON, Stevie, we need a new song, and we need it bad. Give!" That was the kind of appeal Stephen Foster couldn't resist, especially when made by his friend Christy, whose black-face minstrel troupe had already carried many of his songs to fame. So Foster obligingly sat down at his desk, and over-night produced the words and music of *Old Folks at Home*. Christy gave it a high-lighted spot in the show, and audiences who forgot the quips of Mr. Bones and Mr. Interlocutor as soon as their laughter had subsided, hummed "The sun shines bright on my old Kentucky home" for days and weeks after hearing it sung.

It was some time, however, before Stephen received the credit for the song, though he did pocket the cash. The name of Christy appeared on the title-page as author, and for a long time the public believed that Christy had written as well as sung it, especially as he had provided a great many songs for his minstrels. When the truth became known, many were indignant that Foster's thunder should have been stolen, and said it was a shame for Christy to cheat Foster of his rights.

As a matter of fact, Foster had cheated himself. He had requested Christy to suppress his name, because he didn't wish to be typed as a specialist in "Ethiopian melodies," of which he had turned out quite a number. Unquestionably, had he known that his simple little verses would be translated into every known language, and the tune sung, hummed, and whistled all over the world, he would have clung more tenaciously to his title as its author.

SMETANA'S MUSICAL BIOGRAPHY

WHEN THE BOHEMIAN composer, Bědrich Smetana, wrote his string quartet in 1876, he aptly titled it "Aus Meinem Leben." (From My Life.) He related graphically, in music, the events that had shaped him into the great composer of strongly national music. Then, lest the language of music be not understood by everyone, he described its meaning in words. In 1878, six years before his death, he wrote a letter, setting forth the "program" of his musical autobiography.

In the first movement, he dwelt upon his youthful inclination to art, and his strongly romantic tendencies. There was in him, he said, "an unspeakable yearning for something I could not definitely express or definitely imagine, and also a sort of warning of my future disasters." Like many young men of the period (he lived from 1824 to 1884), he tended to exaggerate his emotional states, and to glory somewhat in the gentle melancholy that attended his "unspeakable yearning."

That he possessed a lighter side, he proved in the second movement, a species of polka. In his young and hungry days, he was obliged to write dance music, among other things, for a living, and to dance to it, too, whenever he was invited to do so. Since he danced well, and knew how to make himself agreeable, he was a welcome and popular visitor to the ballrooms of aristocrats. He set down in music his impressions of some of these gatherings, distasteful in many ways to a man of democratic standards. But the chords grew complicated—like his impressions—so that some performers who attempted to play the quartet pronounced this movement "impossible to perform."

They embarked with relief on the Largo Sostenuto—the third movement—a glowing tribute to his first wife, Katerina. She too was a musician, who persuaded her teacher, Prokosch, to take Smetana as a pupil on credit, encouraged him to persist in his musical studies and aided him in the establishment of his conservatory in Prague, where she taught faithfully as his assistant. All of this is between the lines of his music, which is imbued with his love for her.

In the last movement, the mature man turns from personal to national issues. Bohemia had declared her independence. Smetana, director of the new National Opera House in Prague, had written a half-dozen operas, strongly national in character, and an orchestral epic in six cantos, *Ma Vlast* (My Country). His country's rich heritage of folk-song was utilized to the fullest extent by him. He had come to be known as the founder of Czech national music.

But alas! At the height of his career, a catastrophe befell him. He grew deaf, not gradually, like Beethoven, but suddenly and incurably. In the Finale of the quartet, we find a long-sustained note, a shriek of despair, that "fateful whistling of the highest tones in my ear which was announcing my deafness." This is the tragic climax of the quartet, and of his life—the calamity which ended all. A few short years later, he died in a hospital for the insane.

THE WOODEN SHOE
OF PAGANINI

WHEN PAGANINI, the great Italian violinist, lay ill in Paris in the winter of 1832, among his few diversions were the daily visits of Nicette, the peasant girl who came daily to cook and clean and keep his room in order. She was young and pretty and always cheerful. When, one day, she came in silently and went glumly about her work with downcast eyes, Paganini knew something was wrong. He saw that she had been crying. "My child," he asked, "what is it that ails you today?"

At this Nicette burst into fresh tears. Between sobs, she related that she had planned to be married shortly. But her young man's number had been drawn in the military lottery, he was to be conscripted, there would be a war, she was sure that he would be shot and killed, she would never see him again, and so on.

"Why not buy a substitute?" suggested Paganini.

"For 1500 francs!" gasped Nicette. "Where could I find so much money?" Paganini said nothing further, but in his neat script, he made an entry in his note-book. "Think what can be done for poor Nicette."

A few days later, a box arrived, addressed to Paganini. When he unpacked it, a large wooden shoe came to light. "Can this be a present from an admirer?" he gravely asked

Nicette. She said she didn't know. He took it to his room, and worked there for three days with the door closed. When he came out, he held under his arm the wooden shoe, transformed into a violin. A few days later, an advertisement appeared for a New Year's Eve concert, at which the great Paganini promised to play "Five pieces on the violin, five on a wooden shoe."

On New Year's Eve, the concert hall was crowded, as always when Paganini played. After he had performed on his violin with his accustomed brilliance, he took up the shoe. On its four strings, he played an original fantasia, which depicted love's young dream, the call to arms, a battle, grief, love and reunion. It was surprisingly expressive and was received with wild applause.

When the audience had finally gone and only Nicette remained sobbing in her corner, deeply affected by the music, Paganini dried her tears and laid in her lap the two thousand francs earned by the concert. He gave her also the wooden shoe-violin as a souvenir. She later sold it to a collector, bought a military substitute with the francs, and set up housekeeping in style on the remainder of her capital.

AN OLD-WORLD COMPOSER
AND HIS
NEW WORLD SYMPHONY

Anton Dvořák was homesick. He looked out of the window of his study in the National Conservatory of Music upon the sidewalks of New York, its tall buildings, its bustling crowds. In his mind's eye, he saw a different picture:— the village green in a small Bohemian country town, the youths and maidens in picturesque costumes dancing to the gay folk tunes of the village fiddler. There were no fluttering ribbons or whirling skirts on the streets of New York. With a sigh, he realized that he had signed a contract to teach here for four years (1891–95), and homesick or not, here he would have to remain.

There was a knock at the door. One of his favorite students, a young Negro boy, entered. Dvořák and he had often swapped songs, a spiritual for a folksong. Dvořák was much taken with Negro music, in which he said he found the essence of America. Today, the lad brought a tune that was new to Dvořák, and that perfectly suited his mood. The words "Goin' home" and the nostalgic theme found

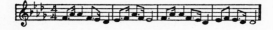

him most receptive to their suggestion. He copied them in his notebook at once, though there was little likelihood of his forgetting them.

Some weeks later, he went for a visit to the town of Spillville, Iowa. Here, he wrote, he found "few people and so much empty space, but the few people were all Czechs." Spillville proved a blessed refuge when his longing for his homeland became unendurable. He settled down for a few weeks' rest, during which he wrote his Symphony, Opus 95, subtitled "From the New World." It was the first work he composed while in the United States, and the theme of the Largo was the spiritual *Goin' Home*, sung for him by his friend.

ENFANT TERRIBLE

WHEN GERALDINE FARRAR sang Madam Butterfly, she always worried over the last scene, in which she appeared with a small child, her son by the errant Pinkerton. It had to be a very passive child, who would submit without protest to being clutched to her bosom, sung to, sobbed over, and finally blindfolded while his mother commited singing suicide. By way of insurance, she insisted that the management have four or five children on hand; when the moment for the big scene arrived, she would select the one that looked promisingly calm. The method worked until one evening when her judgment failed her. She walked out with the little darling in her arms, to hear it emit loud shrieks of fear at sight of the audience. She could not quiet it with whispered endearments nor even whispered threats of punishment. Enraged, she ran to the stage window at which a few minutes earlier, all pathos, she had sung her famous song of waiting. Flinging open the window, she dropped the child through it. The fall did not quiet it, and she finished her scene to the accompaniment of offstage shrieks. A damage suit filed by the indignant parents was the sequel to that performance.

Another great singer, Florence Easton, had difficulties of a different kind in the same role. She was singing *Butterfly* in Germany. Her manager decided to engage a dwarf instead of the usual child actor, but omitted to mention the fact to the prima donna. Dressed in a kimono, and suitably made up, a pretty little boy was placed in Mme. Easton's arms at the proper cue. He cuddled down comfortably with well simulated affection. After she had sung a few bars, she felt a little hand unmistakably caressing her neck. She looked down in astonishment but sang on. The hand continued to explore, amorously and skilfully, and she finished the scene with difficulty. As soon as the curtain had descended, she asked, "My dear child, how old are you?"

A sqeaky little voice piped "Twenty-nine."

SAINT-SAËNS, INCOGNITO

THE COMPOSER Saint-Saëns one day decided to go on a composing spree, a "lost week-end" without alcohol. He simply disappeared without farewell or by-your-leave from the boulevards of Paris, where he was a familiar and well-loved figure. Admirers would follow him on his daily walks, and would whistle or sing bits from his popular writings—a gesture intended as a compliment, but which almost drove him crazy. He felt that he must have peace and privacy. And so he muffled himself theatrically in a long cloak, traveled incognito to the Canary Islands, and rented a room there under an assumed name. Then he settled down to work.

However, he was not unobserved. The eyes of neighbors noted his curious behavior, and spied upon his comings and goings. Word got about that he spent hours seated at a table, making mysterious marks on large sheets of paper which he showed to no-one. The local police became first interested, then suspicious. They took to shadowing him. Saint-Saëns, annoyed, changed his room; then, when the surveillance persisted, he changed it again and yet again. The police, determined to arrest him, awaited him on his doorstep.

Just as he approached the house, a stranger accosted him. "Pardon me," he said, "you are M. Camille Saint-Saëns of Paris, are you not?" The composer was obliged to admit his identity. His incognito was upset—so, too, was the case against him. The police, all smiles and shrugs, bowed themselves out. But the public and the *Danse Macabre* dogged his footsteps for the remainder of his stay.

A JINX OPERA

THE COMPOSER Offenbach devoted his life to writing operettas, designed to divert Napoleon and Eugénie and their pleasure-loving subjects. His was the light touch dear to the French heart. It took ninety operettas and twenty-five years to induce him to ask himself "Why shouldn't I try something more ambitious, perhaps even a grand opera, for a change?" His operetta, *Les Contes d'Hoffman* (Tales of Hoffman), a recounting of the amorous exploits of the Count Hoffman, had been gathering dust for some years on a shelf, after a successful production. "A pretty good operetta," mused the aging Offenbach. "Perhaps an even better grand opera." And he set to work to glorify its pretty tunes into lasting beauty. Death overtook him at sixty-one, when it was practically completed. He never saw it produced, although it eventually proved the major basis of his reputation.

It lay quiescent for a while after his death. Then it came into the hands of Ernest Guiraud, a New Orleans composer, who revised and

partly orchestrated it. Since New Orleans was
the home of grand opera in the New World at
that time, particularly French opera, it was
quite logical for a New Orleans composer to
carry on where Offenbach left off, although it
is proverbially hard luck for several cooks to
mix an operatic broth. When *Les Contes
d'Hoffman* was finally performed at the Opéra
Comique in Paris on Feb. 10, 1881, it was successfully repeated a hundred times within the
year.

Its hard luck actually started the following
December, when it was produced at the Ring-
theatre in Vienna. On the second night of the
run, a disastrous fire swept the theatre, destroy-
ing it completely. Hundreds of lives were lost,
the singers barely escaped, all the costumes,
scenery, and properties were destroyed. For
those who took part in it, *The Tales of Hoffman*
spelt inescapable tragedy, unspeakable horror.
For a long time thereafter, singers refused to
appear in the opera, players to play in the
orchestra. The charred odor of conflagration
hung about it. It became known as a hard-
luck opera, a jinx. To this day, the story of the
conflagration is coupled with its name and,
although much of Offenbach's fame rests upon
it, it continues to be black-listed by those whose
memories survive the intervening years.

THE TWO PRICKLIES

WHEN JOHANNES BRAHMS invited friends, as he often did, to spend an hour with "the two pricklies," he meant first himself, and second, his favorite eating-place, the Red Hedgehog Restaurant in Vienna. Here he was to be found at meal-times whenever he was in Vienna. He loved its dark, smoke-filled room with arched ceilings and heavy woodwork, its Gemütlichkeit, its delicious local foods and wines. Here he swapped stories with boon companions—von Bülow, Johann Strauss, Dvořák, the critic Hanslick, the Beethoven scholar Nottebohm, and many others, who were happy to be recognized members of his "three-hours-for-lunch club."

One day in October, 1889, the composer Anton Brückner was led to the long Stamm- tisch where Brahms and his friends had just seated themselves. The two men knew each other slightly, and knew, too, that they dif- fered diametrically on one of the important questions agitating the musical world at the time:—"Who is Wagner, what is he, that all

our youth adore him?" Brückner was a
reverent disciple of Wagner, for whose person
and music he cherished an unbounded and un-
critical admiration. Brahms, on the other
hand, was anything but enthusiastic about
Wagner. Both the two men and their friends
took this difference of opinion very seriously,
and so they sat uncomfortably at the same
table, stiff and taciturn, like Capulets and
Montagues unwittingly brought together.

Brahms took up the menu to order his
luncheon, and his face cleared. "Ah," he
exclaimed, smacking his lips. "Dumplings
with smoked meat today! That's my favorite
dish!" Brückner broke into a wide smile. "I
say, Dr. Brahms," he exploded happily.
"Dumplings and smoked meat! *That's* where
we two agree!" The ice was broken. Peace
and contentment reigned, and the name of
Wagner was temporarily banished from the
domain of the two pricklies.

BRAHMS' BIRTHDAY
SYMPHONY

It was May 7, 1883. Johannes Brahms stood, frowning, at the high desk in his study in Vienna. Sheets of music-paper were spread before him, the beginnings of a symphony. He didn't like what he had written, and the more he looked, the less he liked it. In a sudden frenzy, he gathered up the papers, crumpled them into a ball, and threw them into the waste paper basket. Resentfully, he glowered at the empty desk, himself feeling equally empty.

"Um Gotteswillen," he exclaimed aloud. "I know what's the matter. Today is my birthday. Fifty! I'm fifty! No wonder I can't write. Haven't I always said that an artist is through at fifty? This proves it. I've nothing more to say, I'll never write another note of music." Then, as a thought struck him, he started to rummage among his correspondence files. "Ah, here it is." He drew out the copy of a letter addressed to Simrock, his publisher. It stated that he had always felt that fifty was the age at which to quit, and that he probably would publish no more after reaching that age. "So that's taken care of," he murmured with rueful satisfaction.

"A good country walk is what I need," he decided, turning his back on the desk which, for all his rationalizing, continued to stare at him reproachfully. "But let me see—I seem to remember something, some engagement. Of course! Here's the memo. I promised to lunch today with the Ehrbars. I almost forgot." He looked down at his patched, faded blue alpaca suit. Insult to injury! He'd have to dress, and how he hated to fuss with clothes! Recalling that a new suit hung in his closet, however, he determined to break it in at once. He dressed himself, grumbling under his breath. Something was wrong. He kept stumbling. Looking down, he found that the tailor had made his trousers several inches too long, so that they trailed on the floor. Petulantly, he seized a pair of shears, and trimmed the offending trouser-legs jaggedly to the desired length. Then he put on his famous coffee-colored top-coat, but it was too heavy for the warm Spring sunshine. Off it came, and in its stead he hung a plaid shawl over his shoulders, pinned it together with a large safety-pin, took the umbrella that always went with him, and thus oddly accoutred, wended his way to the Ehrbars.

They knew him well, and took him as he was, without comment. Their cordial greeting was balm to his soul, as their luncheon was to his stomach. Brahms was a gourmet, but he could find nothing to criticize in the meal of oysters and caviar, cold meats, asparagus fresh from the Ehrbar estate (two bunches to each guest), cheese, dessert, and champagne. Leaning back in his chair in a state of blissful repletion, he asked idly "Did you happen to know that today is my birthday?" "But of course. This party was planned on that account. And since you seem to have enjoyed it, we'll repeat it every year on May 7, with the same menu. Have we your promise?" Brahms was only too happy to comply, and to affirm his pleasure.

By the time he left their good company, his depression of the morning was a thing of the past. He set out for one of the long walks in which he delighted, along the fashionable Prater, and thence to the woods. As he strolled there, alone, beside the Danube, musical ideas began to form in his mind. Faster and faster they came. In his elation he sang aloud "F A F! F A F! My own device. I'll use it as the motto of my new symphony. And F shall be its key." Forgotten were all his resolves to write no more. He whipped his notebook from his pocket and wrote as fast as he could, eager to capture on paper the musical thoughts crowding upon him. This was the beginning of his third symphony, often called his *Eroica*, paralleling Beethoven's Third. He worked on it for some time in Vienna, and finished it during the summer months in Wiesbaden. And so the triumphant F Major Symphony No. III came to life. Far from being "finished" at fifty, Brahms lived to be sixty-four, and to write still another symphony.

THE REVOLT OF
HUGO WOLF

WHEN HUGO WOLF was a boy, studying like all good German boys in the Gymnasium (high school) he tried to console himself for the time spent with hated studies by stealing every moment possible to run to the conservatory. Religious services and Sunday sermons were one part of the school curriculum which he regularly avoided, since little or no music was included in the service. Instead, he went to the local church, listened avidly to the Masses sung by the choir, and played the violin in the little orchestra there whenever there was an empty place for him.

One day, old Zager, one of the teachers at the school, saw fit to reprimand him for missing Sunday Mass at school. Hugo listened quietly, without defending himself. This enraged the professor, who burst into a tirade against "that damned music." The young man's calm deserted him. He flew like a panther at the defamer of his holy of holies, giving him angry

word for word, blow for blow. Had a fellow
student not dragged him away, shaking with
rage, the outcome might have been grave. As
it was, Wolf received a black mark in conduct,
and a blacker one in religious studies, and
shook the dust of the school from his feet in a
cloud, while making a bee-line from the
school-room to the conservatory.

COMPOSITION BY TELEPATHY

ONE SUNSHINY DAY, when the out-of-doors was more than usually inviting, Edvard Grieg embarked on a rowboat excursion with his friend Beyer. He dabbled his hand in the cooling waters of his native fiord, and relaxed blissfully. A musical idea was wafted to him by his patron saint. What could he do? What would any composer do under the same circumstances? He whipped out manuscript paper, and wrote down the theme. He laid the paper on the bench beside him. Along came a playful gust of wind, seized the paper, and blew it away into the water.

It was riding peacefully on top of a wave when Beyer glimpsed it, recalled a white flash going past his line of vision. He leaned over the side and fished it out. He read it silently, without comment from the luxuriously relaxing Grieg. He put it in his pocket. After a judicious interval, he whistled the theme, softly, meditatively, one eye on Grieg. Grieg jumped.

He turned pale. "What in the world is it that you're whistling?" he stammered. Beyer replied, with exaggerated detachment, "Oh, just a little thing that came into my head." "The devil!" exclaimed Grieg, "I had exactly the same idea a few minutes ago."

HE LAUGHS BEST

LEONCAVALLO dearly loved to listen to people's comments on his operas, and whenever possible, he slipped into the theatre after the curtain had risen, trusting that, in the darkened house, his identity might remain unknown.

One evening, when his *Pagliacci* was being performed in the little town of Forli, he found himself seated next to a girl who clapped with immense enthusiasm. Between claps, she frowned at the gentleman beside her, who applauded not at all. "Don't you like it?" she whispered when she could apparently bear it no longer. "No. It's terrible," replied the composer. "I'm sorry I came." "Really?" with incredulity. "Really," with an inward chuckle. "If that's your opinion, you know nothing about music," snapped the girl. "Just listen," countered Leoncavallo. "Stolen themes, all stolen. That last one was from Bizet, the one before from Beethoven. There isn't an original idea in the whole opera." She turned her back without a word and from then on ignored him completely.

At breakfast the next morning, he found the local newspaper open on his plate. Large headlines stared at him: "Leoncavallo On His Opera *Pagliacci*." The lady reporter who had sat beside him had blown up their little exchange into a long interview, quoting him verbatim. It was publicity for him and his opera, but hardly of the sort he would have chosen. Wryly, he admitted to himself that hers was the last laugh—and the best.

◇◇◇◇◇◇◇◇◇◇◇◇◇◇◇◇◇◇◇◇◇◇◇◇◇◇

A SULLIVANISM
MINUS GILBERT

A COMMISSION to write incidental music for a play was offered to Arthur Sullivan, of Gilbert and Sullivan fame. He declined with thanks. "The fact is," he said, "that music in the theatre is a mistake. When the curtain is up, music disturbs the actors, and when the curtain is down, it disturbs the audience."

DEAR PERCY GRAINGER

In the late 1890's, Edvard Grieg, the Norwegian pianist-composer, and Percy Grainger, the Australian ditto, ditto, summered in Norway and struck up an unusual friendship. They walked, talked and boated for hours together. They turned each other's pages at the piano and played each other's music superbly. The fastidious Grieg loved his "dear Percy Grainger" for himself, although that self embodied eccentricities of a high order. Grainger, for his part, when Grieg died, mourned him deeply. He took the watch Mrs. Grieg presented as a keepsake, fastened it to his belt-strap with an old frayed piece of sting, and stuck it in a side pocket of his trousers. For him to wear it at all was a tremendous concession.

Many of the eccentricities which Grieg loved in him were known to all. Grainger never walked when he could run, and never rode when he could walk. He walked to his concert engagements, and frequently arrived, when on tour, just in time for the concert, in a completely disheveled condition, carrying his evening clothes in an antique grip. Sometimes he wore them on the train, covered with a white satin-lined evening cape, from the pocket of which he would produce his toothbrush, a packet of sandwiches, or a roll of manuscript, as the need arose.

One day, he had to go to play a concert in Wausau, Wisconsin. For the exercise, he walked from his home in White Plains to New York City for the train. It was a long trip, and he wore his usual shabby suit, carried his grip, and traveled by day-coach. He improved the shining hour of travel by working.

He wrote steadily, crumpling up papers as he discarded ideas and throwing them on the floor. The conductor eyed him with suspicion. When the train arrived, Percy emerged from a sea of crumpled papers, blinking dazedly and completely exhausted. The conductor made no protest when the local policeman at the railroad station arrested him as a suspicious character. He was haled before the chief of police, who was justly annoyed because he was planning to attend the Grainger concert and didn't wish to be late. "What's your name?" asked the chief impatiently. "Percy Grainger." "Oh yeah," retorted the chief mockingly, "Well, if yours is Percy Grainger, mine is William Tell." Grainger accepted this item of information matter-of-factly, and permitted himself to be booked for vagrancy and led without protest to the jail. Here he settled himself comfortably in a cell, ate some of the hardtack and cheese he always carried with him, unpacked his grip, and cheerfully dressed for the concert. He was ready to go when the concert committee arrived, complete with an apologetic chief of police, to rectify the error and conduct him to the concert hall. He never played a better performance. Dear Percy Grainger!

RIMSKY-KORSAKOFF, REV-
OLUTIONARY ARISTOCRAT

ON A DAY IN 1905, the Conservatory of St.
Petersburg was surrounded by a milling crowd
—students on strike, ten or twelve non-strikers
trying to cross the picket-line, and a cordon of
police on horse and foot, pushing strikers and
bystanders about indiscriminately in a vague
effort to keep the peace. The scene, familiar
enough today, was then comparatively strange.

Rimsky-Korsakoff, the composer, was a professor of composition at the Conservatory.
Although a member of the ruling class in Russia, he was of strong democratic sympathies,
and had done his best to prevent this outbreak
of violence. The students had determined
upon self-government as a means of correcting
some of the injustices of the directors of the
Conservatory, and Rimsky-Korsakoff approved of their plan. As a member of a committee to adjust the differences between them
and the directors, he championed the students
and was immediately accused of being the
leader of a revolutionary movement. He advised closing the school until the differences
could be arbitrated, but the directors decided

to close for a few days only, an empty gesture.
When the doors were opened, violence ensued,
and the students were strengthened thereby in
their determination to fight for their rights.

In a carefully worded letter, Rimsky-
Korsakoff enumerated some of their griev-
ances. He pointed out that the musical artists
were subordinate to the Director; that the
Director was irremovable, and could and did
consider himself a dictator; that the directorate
as a whole was indifferent to the fate of the
students and the quality of the education they
received, and so on. At a meeting of the Art
Council the letter created an uproar. The
Conservatory was closed again, more than a
hundred students were expelled outright,
others were suspended and several directors
resigned. Shortly thereafter Rimsky-Korsakoff was dismissed from his post by the board
of directors, without consultation with the
Art Council. In retaliation, the composer
wrote a letter to one of the leading newspapers,
in which he minced no words and followed
this action by resigning from the St. Petersburg
branch of the Musical Society. The reaction
of the public was as gratifying as it was unexpected. He became a hero. Letters, deputa-
tions, and laudatory comment came to him
from remote corners of Russia. More of the
directors were compelled by public pressure to
relinquish their positions.

The students then decided, partly as a protest, partly as an artistic enterprise, to present his opera *Kashchey* and some of his other works at a gala concert. The opera was already in rehearsal, so a date was set, and it was performed before a large audience. After the last curtain, there were repeated calls for the composer and impassioned speeches were made, punctuated by shouts of "Down with the autocracy." So unrestrained was the demonstration that it was thought best not to continue the performance with the concert which had been scheduled to follow.

For several months, the name of Rimsky-Korsakoff was spoken in St. Petersburg in whispers. The police were ordered to prevent any presentation of his works there. On the other hand, his compositions appeared with daring frequency in concerts outside the proscribed area. Although his classes at the Conservatory could not be resumed since the institution was closed, many students came to work with him privately. He was kept so busy that he found it impossible to settle down to writing music, but embarked instead on a textbook of orchestration which became a must for incipient composers. And as the political excitement subsided he found himself increasingly honored, not alone as one of Russia's leading composers but as one of her beloved revolutionaries.

SLEZAK'S ROYAL CROWN

THE OPERA COMPANY was about to entrain in the station at Vienna, en route for a long tour. There was the usual hustle and bustle, with wardrobe trunks piled high waiting to be loaded on the train under the anxious eye of the stars' valets and maids. The stars themselves, meanwhile, took their ease in their own compartments.

Leo Slezak, the famous tenor, had just arranged himself and his belongings comfortably, when his valet, Franz, appeared with a large brown paper package carefully tied with string. He handed the package to Slezak. "I'm sorry, Sir. This wouldn't fit in the trunk. So I left it out, to be carried separately." Slezak was not pleased. In the package was the golden crown he wore as the Prophet in Meyerbeer's opera of that title. It was easily bent, its paste jewels were not too firmly set, and he wished it to blaze in all its glory when he needed it. Like the resourceful man he was, he took down one of his wife's many hat-boxes, tossed out the hat it contained and tenderly ensconced the crown in its place. The hat remained in Vienna.

Towards evening, the train approached the border and the inevitable inspection for dutiable articles had to be undergone. Slezak made the routine declaration, "Nothing to declare." "Nothing at all?" "Nothing." "What is in that box? Kindly open it." Inwardly cursing, but outwardly all amiability, he raised the lid and lifted out the crown. When the inspector saw the shining stones, his eyes bulged. He stepped back and saluted respectfully. "Thank you kindly, your Highness. I trust your Highness will forgive my having inconvenienced you. Pass, your Highness."

DONE TO DEATH

SERGEI RACHMANINOFF and his friend, the American composer, Abram Chasins, were telling each other their troubles. Chasins complained, "No matter what I write—and I write a great deal—I keep hearing my *Three Chinese Pieces for Piano*, and *Rush Hour in Hongkong*. I'm sick of them. I simply can't escape them." "Ah," said Rachmaninoff, smiling one of his enigmatic smiles, "the *Three Chinese Pieces* are your *C# Minor Prelude*."

The *C# Minor Prelude* is the piece which Ernest Newman described as "It." Rachmaninoff wrote it when he was twenty. He thought little of it and was astounded when its crashing chords were applauded, not only in Russia but everywhere. He was further astounded and not too pleased, when "It" went on a goodwill tour ranging all over the world, making his name known, while his *First Piano Concerto* and *First Symphony* were being coolly received in Russia. But the *C# Minor Prelude* and the name of Rachmaninoff continued to be married, however he strove to divorce them. And to this day, when the name of Rachmaninoff is mentioned, faces brighten and the automatic response is "Ah yes, the composer of the *C# Minor Prelude*."

Paderewski's equally hackneyed *Minuet*, which was conceived in a spirit of good clean fun, irked him no less in his day. As a young pianist in Warsaw, he visited often at the home of Dr. Chalubinski, a passionate devotee of the music of Mozart. At the time, the young man had in his repertoire only three or four Mozart works. These he was obliged to repeat again and again, to the never-ending rapture of the good Doctor and his friends. But in time Paderewski became bored with this undiscriminating Mozart worship. He decided to give the Doctor a lesson. One evening, just for fun, he sat down at his piano at home, and improvised a Minuet in the style of Mozart.

The next time he visited the Doctor, in response to the usual request for "a little Mozart, please," he played his own Minuet. The response was even better than he had anticipated. "Marvelous, indescribable!" cried the host. "Tell me, Paderewski, tell me honestly, is there anyone now alive who could write such music?" "Yes, Doctor, there is." "There is? Who?" "It is I." "Impossible. I am surprised at your effrontery. How dare you say such a thing?" "But I wrote the

Minuet you have just been hearing." The Doctor simply could not believe it. After Paderewski had finally convinced him that the *Minuet* was actually his own, relations were somewhat strained. There was no more music that evening. However, at the next session, the friendly atmosphere was restored, and Paderewski's Minuet took its place with Mozart's in the affections of the old gentlemen. Its later history is well known. The many pupils of Paderewski's teacher, Leschetitzky, took it up enthusiastically. Leschetitzky's wife, Mme. Essipoff, played it persistently at her concerts. It was published and sold widely to amateurs. And it was dinned in Paderewki's ears until he heartily wished he never had written it.

A MUSICIAN OF TOMORROW

DEBUSSY AND a few friends were having a quiet evening at home. On Debussy's table lay a new book by Romain Rolland, *Musiciens d'- Aujourdhui* (Musicians of Today). It contained critical sketches of contemporary composers, including, of course, Debussy. When the discussion turned to the chapter about him, Debussy said nothing, frowned as if displeased. "Don't you like it?" "Yes, of course I do. But I feel that I don't belong in this book. I am not a musician of today, but a musician of tomorrow and the next day and the days after that. Why can't I be put where I belong?"

PITY THE TEACHER

A TEACHER IN A conservatory of music once remarked sadly that in his school, contrary to custom, the walls had ears, while the pupils were sound-proof.

It was probably in that conservatory that Hans von Bülow, a somewhat irascible teacher, was giving a piano lesson one day. His pupil made more than her quota of mistakes. His comment on her performance was, "Ach Gott, you play the easy passages with a difficulty that is simply enormous!"

SONATA MADE TO ORDER

MISCHA AND "Papa" Elman were guests at a musicale, at which Georges Enesco was also present. As a compliment to the distinguished composer, Jacques Gordon played Enesco's First Violin Sonata, and was loudly applauded. "Papa" Elman fidgeted, listened, fidgeted, listened. Finally he plucked the composer's sleeve. "Listen, Maestro, will you write a violin sonata for my Mischa?" he asked. A few minutes later, "Maestro, I beg you to write a violin sonata for my Mischa." Later still, more urgently "I tell you, you *must* write a violin sonata for my Mischa." Enesco smiled his gentle smile, and said nothing. "Papa" beamed at what he assumed to be his assent.

The next day, Enesco had tea with the Elmans. He brought with him a photostat of his *Second Sonata for Violin*, which was still in manuscript. He had just completed it, after working at it for many months, and was well pleased that his labors were at an end. "Papa" Elman pounced upon the photostat, held it aloft, and asked naïvely, "And is this the sonata you have written for my Mischa?"— only twenty-four hours after placing his order!

KREISLER'S "MUSICAL HOAX"

WHEN FRITZ KREISLER, the great violinist, was a comparatively unknown young man on the threshold of a career, he decided that what violin recital programs needed was some new blood. Having dutifully practiced all the stock pieces and played them in public most satisfactorily, he viewed with distaste a long career devoted to playing and re-playing those same pieces. So he decided to write some of his own. Since he was as fine a composer as he was a violinist, this was well within his scope.

At a concert in Vienna in 1905, he introduced into the program three new pieces— *Liebesfreud* (The Joy of Love), *Liebesleid* (The Pain of Love), and *Schön Rosmarin* (Beautiful Rosmarin). They are charming short works, now almost hackneyed, thanks to many performances and recordings by Kreisler and others. At their première, they created a sensation. Their composer allowed them to be attributed to Joseph Lanner, a composer who had died a half-century previously, but whose music was still loved and revered by the

Viennese. On the same program, however, he also placed his *Caprice Viennois*, to which he affixed his own name. The day after the concert, the critics of Vienna fell upon him. They made scathing remarks about the young artist's impudence in placing a piece of his own side by side with works of the great Lanner. They compared the *Caprice Viennois* unfavorably with *Liebesfreud* etc. In self-defense, Kreisler was obliged to acknowledge his authorship of all four pieces. Then the critics were chagrined and abashed. The discovery that they had been hoaxed caused them to feel not at all kindly disposed to Kreisler. They couldn't deny that he was a great fiddler, but they preferred to forget that he aspired to be a composer as well.

At that time, Kreisler had no thought of publishing these works, or the others which he quietly added to his repertoire from time to time. But as they became increasingly popular, and shouts from the audience of *Liebesfreud*, *Liebesleid* sounded insistently during the encore section at his concerts, his friends urged him not to keep them to himself, but to grant other fiddlers an opportunity to play them. Finally he consented to the publication of the original four, with the proviso that every copy must contain a notice of Kreisler's authorship "in a measure confessed." Even this did not open

the ears of the public and critics to his authorship of other pieces, which he had presented
from time to time as transcriptions of works
by famous composers of the past.   His list
attained good proportions.

CONCERTO IN C MAJOR	*Vivaldi-Kreisler*
ALLEGRETTO IN G MINOR	*Porpora-Kreisler*
ANDANTINO	*Padre Martini-Kreisler*
AUBADE PROVENÇALE	*Couperin-Kreisler*
CHANSON LOUIS XII	*Couperin-Kreisler*
LA CHASSE	*Cartier-Kreisler*
MENUET	*Porpora-Kreisler*
PRAELUDIUM AND ALLEGRO	*Pugnani-Kreisler*
LA PRÉCIEUSE	*Couperin-Kreisler*
PREGHIERA	*Padre Martini-Kreisler*
SCHERZO	*Dittersdorf-Kreisler*
SICILIENNE AND RIGAUDON	*Francoeur-Kreisler*
STUDY ON A CHORAL	*Stamitz-Kreisler*
TEMPO DI MENUETTO	*Pugnani-Kreisler*

Critics continued to delight in discussions of
the style of Padre Martini as ¬evealed in the
Andantino, or of Porpora as set forth in the
Allegretto, with hardly a word for Kreisler as
the transcriber.

Finally, in 1935, Olin Downes, music critic
of the New York *Times*, undertook to track
down the changes Kreisler had made in
transcribing the beautiful Pugnani-Kreisler
Praeludium and Allegro.   Cornered, Kreisler

was forced to admit that he had never seen a *Praeludium and Allegro* by Pugnani, but had written the whole thing himself, with regard for the style in which Pugnani *might* have written it. His admission created a storm. He was accused of robbing dead composers of their justly-earned laurels in order to add to his own, of cheating the public, of being down-right dishonest. It was one thing to write under a pseudonym, like Josef Hofmann, whose works were played under the unknown name of Dvorsky, but who readily admitted that they were his. It was quite another to masquerade as a Vivaldi or a Couperin in modern dress. A few people grinned and said that Kreisler had played a good joke. But they were in the minority. Finally Kreisler, bewildered by all the to-do, explained: "Necessity forced this course on me thirty years ago, when I was desirous of enlarging my programs. I found it inexpedient and tactless to repeat my name endlessly on programs. . . . In informed circles there was in those days not the slightest doubt about the authorship of my pieces. At no time was there any thought of publishing them."

Gradually the furore abated. And gradually the public came to feel that "any composer, living or dead, should be proud to claim these works as his own."

THE "GREATEST VIOLINIST IN THE WORLD"

ONE EVENING, Jascha Heifetz and Mischa Elman were dining together. The fact that both were renowned violinists did not prevent their amiable enjoyment of each other's company. Elman had, as usual, been holding forth on the success of his recently completed tour—sold-out houses, autograph hunters, recording contracts, etc. Finally, noting that Heifetz had been silent for some time, he said genially, "But enough about me, Jascha. Let's talk about you. Tell me, what did you think of my last concert?"

At this point, a messenger approached their table with a letter on a silver salver. "I beg your pardon, gentlemen. I have a letter here for one of you, but I don't know which one." "To whom is it addressed?" "To the 'greatest violinist in the world.'" The gentlemen looked deprecatory. "For you," said Heifetz graciously. "Oh no, for you," faltered Mischa without conviction. Heifetz, "I insist."

Mischa, "I couldn't." This went on for several minutes, while the page stood uncertainly by, still holding the letter. Finally, Heifetz tossed him a coin, and he placed the letter on the table. "What do we do now?" asked Heifetz wryly. "Let's open it together," suggested Elman. "That's the only way to find out for whom it is intended." Accordingly, one slit the envelope, the other drew out the letter. Both bent over it, then burst out laughing. The letter started, "My dear Mr. Kreisler."

BREAKFAST IS SERVED

MISCHA ELMAN, violinist of the sonorous tone, and his accompanist Sanford Schluessel, both of them short of stature, plump, and blondish, were on tour. They had the luxury suite in their Pullman, traveled in what the French call "le comfort moderne."

The first day out, Mischa slept late. Sanford, however, went reasonably early to the diner, where he was overwhelmed with attentions. A magnificent breakfast was set before him, beginning with honeydew melon, proceeding through cereal, bacon and eggs, to culminate in griddle cakes, cinnamon buns and coffee. Every once in so often, the head-waiter appeared, employing the usual hand-rubbing-bowing technique, to inquire anxiously if everything was quite all right. Schluessel graciously reassured him on that point, signed Mischa's name to the check, as he always did, and returned to the suite full-fed and well content.

In due time, Elman arose, dressed, and hied him to the diner. In presto time, he returned, fuming. "Such a rotten breakfast! Such rotten service! Why didn't you tell me? It's a disgrace that any artist should be treated this way. I shan't travel on this line again. Nothing much to eat, and everything cold! It's terrible."

"Why, what's the matter?" inquired Schluessel innocently.

"Matter? Everything is the matter, as I've just been telling you. I shall write a letter to the railroad. Tell me, did you have such a terrible breakfast?"

"Mine was good."

"Good! I don't believe it."

"But it was. Unusually good, and plenty of it, too."

Elman decided to investigate. In short order he learned that the head waiter, mistaking the accompanist for the artist, had lavished upon Schluessel all the attentions designed for Elman, and had bestowed upon the virtuoso the cold hospitality considered good enough for a lesser artist. It was a lesson in social behavior not to be disregarded. Nor, to Mr. Elman's credit be it said, did he fail to see the point.

PSYCHOLOGICAL TEMPERATURE

THE PIANIST Leopold Godowsky, the violinist Mischa Elman, and some fellow-artists were seated together in a box at a Heifetz recital in Carnegie Hall. Heifetz played superbly, as always, and the enthusiasm of the audience mounted steadily. Elman grew more and more uneasy. He twisted on his chair, stood up, sat down, fidgeted and twiddled. Finally, he drew his handkerchief from his pocket, wiped his perspiring brow, and whispered loudly to Godowsky, "Don't you think it's terribly hot here?" "Not for pianists," was the barbed reply.

INFORMATION PLEASE

A CHILD ASKED his father, "Daddy, is the *Harp Quartet* of Beethoven called that because it's for four harps?

"Certainly not," replied the father. "Schubert's *Trout Quintet* isn't for five trout, is it?"

PADEREWSKI'S THREE B'S

ALL HIS LIFE the pianist Paderewski had a psychological complex against giving a concert in Berlin. There was a good reason for this. When he was a young man, he was engaged to play one of the Beethoven concertos there with the Berlin Philharmonic Orchestra under von Bülow.

From the audience side of the footlights, the occasion appeared a perfectly normal one. On the performers' side, however, nerves were on edge. Von Bülow was in a wretched temper. He had wished to engage another pianist—a charming lady, no doubt—and argued in vain against Paderewski. Even the brilliance of the artist's talent did not dispel his irritation. In insidious ways known to the initiated, he did what he could to sabotage the soloist's performance without detracting from his own. Nevertheless, it went well enough until the cadenza. At this point, the conductor usually lays down his baton and listens with at least the appearance of admiration to the soloist until he has to cue the orchestra to play. Von Bülow laid down his baton, and

edged over toward the piano. There he was
seized with a coughing spell, an obviously
intentional one. Turning toward the keyboard, he coughed loudly, maliciously, off
the beat, throwing the already distracted
pianist quite out of rhythm.

Paderewski got through the performance
somehow, and as soon as it was over, rushed
from the building. He flung himself into a

cab outside. "Where to?" asked the cabby. "Anywhere," replied his fare gloomily. The man took a look at the nimbus of red hair atop the uncovered head. "We'll go to the barber," he announced decidedly. That was the last straw. Paderewski didn't go to the barber, nor in all his long and brilliant career would he consent to play a concert in Berlin. Berlin, Bülow and barber were three B's to be avoided.

◇◇◇◇◇◇◇◇◇◇◇◇◇◇◇◇◇◇◇◇◇◇◇◇◇◇◇◇◇

NAME, PLEASE

A LADY WITH an autograph book in her hand gushed up to a distinguished conductor. "Oh, Dr. Koussevitzky, I do so want your autograph," she said. She eagerly opened her book. "Look here, I have Stokowski and Toscanini and Fritz Reiner. Will you sign here?"

"You have all those?" replied Koussevitzky. "That's enough then, you certainly don't need mine." And he turned his back on the lady.

LEAVE TO COMPOSE

RICHARD STRAUSS, like other conductors, had the problem of placing gifted younger men where they could secure experience and an income simultaneously. To his delight, after much negotiation, he succeeded in placing one of his protegés in a big opera house where he hoped that, after serving an apprenticeship, the young man would work himself into a permanent position.

After a few months, the young conductor came to see him. Strauss greeted him cordially. "How are things going?" he inquired. "Fine, fine," replied the young man. "I've just asked for a year's leave of absence." "A year's leave of absence! What for?" "Why, to complete my opera!" "What!" exclaimed Strauss. "A leave of absence because of your opera! But the day has twenty-four hours, twelve for work, eight for sleep. That leaves a good four hours a day for composing. With so much time on your hands, do you mean to tell me that you have to ask for a leave of absence?"

HOME ON THE RANGE

In 1908, John Lomax, folksong collector by appointment to the Library of Congress, was roaming about on and off the range, in search of American folksongs. All he carried with him was a burning enthusiasm, plus a very crude Edison recording machine.

In San Antonio, Texas, he heard of a Negro who had once followed the Old Chisholm Trail as a cook. "Lead me to him," he commanded. He found the old man in his cabin, quite willing to sing for so sympathetic a listener. Lomax set up his machine and selected a chair in the shadow, where his presence would not be too much noticed. He waited, listening silently, while with half-closed eyes the gray-haired Negro sang one song after another. Most of them Lomax already knew, but he was accustomed to that. Folksong collecting is a waiting game. Towards evening, without warning, the old man quavered into "Home, home on the range, where the deer and the antelope play." He produced several verses and chorus. Here was one that Lomax had not run across. He asked for it several times over, while he recorded it and took down the words.

When his first collection of folksongs was published in 1910, it contained the words and music of *Home on the Range*. Nobody paid much attention to it, nor to the other songs in the book, except other folksong enthusiasts. But suddenly, in 1933, Franklin D. Roosevelt heard it somewhere and loved it. Later he declared that it was his favorite song. Overnight it became well-known, everyone's property, truly a people's song, made in America. There was no copyright on it, and professional singers used it on records, radio and concert programs, at night clubs and parties and family gatherings. It had come to stay at the invitation of John Lomax, seconded by F. D. R.

WHEN THE *RITE OF SPRING* WENT WRONG

IGOR STRAVINSKY, Russian composer, was in Paris, completing a ballet, *The Fire-Bird*. His mind was full of the Russian fairy-tale of captive princesses rescued by a bird with fiery plumage from the evil spell of the enchanter Kostchei. He himself cannot explain how it came about that an entirely different picture popped into his mind direct from the pages of Frazer's book, *The Golden Bough*. He found himself thinking vividly of a pagan ceremony celebrating the advent of Spring. In his mind's eye, he saw a beautiful young girl selected by priests as a human sacrifice, saw her dance in a circle of priests and pagans until, growing gradually weaker, she finally dropped in death. The picture tormented him. Nothing was more natural than for him, as a composer, to set down the music inspired by his vision. He wrote it as a ballet, and called it *Le Sacre du Printemps* (The Rite of Spring).

On May 28, 1913, a brilliant audience gathered in the Théâtre des Champs Elysées, in Paris, to witness the first performance.

Pierre Monteux conducted the orchestra, the
dancer Nijinsky was the choreographer, the
scenery and costumes had been designed by
Stravinsky's friend, Nicholas Roerich, and to
make the auspices wholly happy, Diaghilev,
the great impresario of the Ballet Russe, was
in charge of the production. It should have
been one of those world premières that make
history.

It did make history, but not as it was intended. For after the first few bars, the conservatives in the audience made up their minds
that they didn't like the music. From snicker-
ing they proceeded to laughing aloud, to
catcalls, whistling, and a crescendo of jeers that
drowned out the music. Others indignantly
tried to hush them, but insistent requests to
"Sit down in front" only added to the uproar.
Diaghilev had the electric lights flashed on and
off like stop-and-go signals, thinking this would
quiet the hecklers, but they were not to be
subdued. Nijinsky, standing on a chair in
the wings, counted aloud at the top of his
lungs to prompt the dancers. They could not
hear him for the din, nor could they hear the
orchestra, which continued to go through the
motions of playing. The whole effect was that
of a nightmare, with the orchestra straining a
voice from which no audible sound issued,
with dancers gyrating in a rhythm uncon-
nected with the music, with fainting women

being carried out of the auditorium, and the audience, like a lot of satyrs, capering about completely out of hand. The composer left the scene early in the evening. As a result of the shock, he afterwards spent six weeks in a sanatorium.

The trouble, in a nutshell, was that Stravinsky had conceived music that depicted primitive emotions all too well. The barbaric rhythms, clashing discords and wild melody aroused in the listeners elemental emotions they were ashamed to acknowledge. So they deplored the composer's disregard of conventional forms and belittled the very qualities in the music, "coldly mystical and calculatingly savage by turns," that made it an original creation, possibly a work of genius. Critics were no less caustic than laymen, though they had opportunities to revise their judgment at other performances in Paris. The British, oddly enough, received it more sympathetically than their supposedly more tolerant neighbors across the Channel.

The *Sacre* came into its own a year later, when Monteux conducted a performance in concert form, without the ballet. This time the piece had an intelligent appraisal, some of the critics had the grace to swallow the hard words previously uttered, and today it has found its place as program music for the concert hall.

PRIMITIVE PIECE

IN A THEATRE LOBBY in Rio de Janeiro, an orchestra was playing for the entertainment of patrons entering or leaving the performance, or strolling about. The cellist's seat was occupied by young Hector Villa-Lobos, who was something of a character. He had gone into the South American jungles and collected folksongs from the primitive people in hidden villages. He had a peculiar way of composing music, in which he not only embodied these folksongs but used graphs, which he harmonized. Later in his career, he actually orchestrated the sky-line of New York, and the piece was performed at the World's Fair in New York in 1940. But we anticipate. At the time of this story, 1919, Villa-Lobos was known to his companions in the orchestra chiefly as a cellist who occasionally composed pieces which they enjoyed playing.

One of the strollers in the lobby on this particular evening was the pianist Artur Rubinstein, then on tour in South America. When the orchestra broke into one of the young

cellist's tunes, Rubinstein pricked up his ears.
Here was a new voice, an arresting musical
speech. "I don't know that work. What is
it? Who is the composer?" he asked the conductor. Villa-Lobos was hauled, blushing,
from his cellist's chair, and was duly presented.
The pianist complimented him, praised the
work he had heard, asked if there were others.
"Sure," replied Hector, struck almost dumb
by the unexpected appreciation. "Will you
bring them to my room at the hotel later? I'd
like to see and hear them. Please do." Hector nodded, with no intention of going. Later
in the evening, however, he received an urgent
telephone call from Rubinstein, renewing the
invitation. He could not refuse. He presented himself and the full orchestra in the
hotel room and played far into the night.

The visit had results most agreeable for him,
for Rubinstein sang his praises widely and so
effectively that, in 1922, the young man was
subsidized to go to Paris for further study and
stimulation. A wealthy Brazilian footed the
bills. In Paris, the pianist led the composer to
his own publisher, sat down on the piano stool
and devoted an entire afternoon to playing the
works of Villa-Lobos. The latter hesitated
not a moment to sign the contract inspired by
Rubinstein's performance.

In evidence of his appreciation, Villa-Lobos

produced a magnificent piece for the piano, which he dedicated to Rubinstein. He called it *Rudepoêma* (Primitive Piece), and sent it to his friend in 1926 with the following letter:

"My devoted friend,

I do not know whether or not I have been able to put all your spirit into this Rudepoêma, but it is my sincere belief that I have caught your temperament and put its true image upon paper, as a camera might. So, if I have succeeded, it is indeed you who are the true author of this work."

Some time later, the Rudepoêma was re-written as a symphony, but not until it had been widely played as a piano piece by the guardian angel to whom it was dedicated.

CHAVEZ OF MEXICO

BACK IN THE 1930's, the Mexican composer
Carlos Chavez sat, chuckling delightedly, in
a New York theatre. He was attending a performance of *Pins and Needles*, a revue put on by
members of the International Ladies' Garment
Workers' Union. This was the kind of thing
he loved. It was bright and entertaining, it
had social significance, it had "It." The music
was by Harold Rome, a brilliant and at the
time unknown young worker-composer. Act-
ing, sets, costumes, were by members of the
Union, most of whose working time had to be
spent earning their daily bread pushing a
needle. *Needles and Pins* was their relaxation.

Chavez was enchanted by the revue. At
the end of the performance, he raced down the
aisle to meet Harold Rome, who was playing
the piano which, for economic reasons, substituted for an orchestra. Vigorously, he
pumped his hand. Heartily, he congratulated
him, urged him to continue his efforts on be-
half of people's music. This was no superficial
demonstration. For Chavez, who is part

Indian, part Spanish, and by that token wholly Mexican, had previously demonstrated a live interest in workers and their works. He had written a powerful composition, *Llamadas*, for small orchestra and chorus, which had been sung by workers' groups at union meetings at the Casa del Pueblo (People's House) in Mexico City, to a wildly enthusiastic, singing-along audience.

Chavez rescored the work for a large orchestra with chorus. Diego Rivera, the People's Painter in Mexico, a close friend of Chavez, told the authorities in Mexico City how good *Llamadas* was, and how much the people liked it. As a result, when the Palacio dei Bellas Artes (Palace of Fine Arts), which is the official heart of Mexican culture, was dedicated in Mexico City, *Llamadas* was the composition chosen to speak for music. It turned back to the past, to Mexican history and Indian folklore. It looked ahead to a new, life-giving future which combined both, with an additional something. It epitomized Chavez' painstaking research into native music, his collecting of Indian and Aztec musical instruments, and above all, his interest in children and workers.

OL' MAN RIVER

PAUL ROBESON probably recalls with tenderness the day when, an unknown young man who could sing, he appeared in the part of a shabby New Orleans cotton hand in the musical play, *Showboat*, and raised his great voice in the song, *Old Man River*. That song became his very own.

When Jerome Kern, the composer, read Edna Ferber's novel, *Showboat*, he couldn't eat or sleep until he had met the authoress and secured her permission to have her book dramatized, and then to set it to music. It inspired him to write beautiful melodies, of which *Ol' Man River* was perhaps the best. To find the right man to sing it became an obsession with Kern, since the part itself was too insignificant to offer to a star. Alexander Woollcott, who knew Robeson, suggested that Kern come along up to Harlem and hear him. Kern jumped into a taxi without delay, and climbed the stairs of Robeson's flat two at a time. He played the piano accompaniment on a battered upright, while Paul read the song from manuscript. Kern hardly dared believe his ears, and jubilantly insisted that his find come right down with him and sing the song for Oscar Hammerstein, who had written the words. Paul turned to his wife for taxi fare. She offered him a one-way dollar. "Ah go on, Essie," he kidded. "Give me two!" He got the two dollars and, what is more, he got the part.

Production was delayed for two years. Finally opening night arrived. Edna Ferber was so sure the show would flop that she couldn't bear to go. But at the last moment, neither could she bear to stay away.

When Robeson sang "Ol' Man River" she found herself carried away by it, and forgetful of her own part in the performance, she joined the others in the crowded house in applauding till her gloves split and her arms ached. When the other actors tried to go on with the show, their lips moved, but no sound seemed to come forth. It was Robeson the audience demanded, and Robeson appeared, to bow again and again, and to sing encore after encore. He was to carry the song all over Europe on later tours.

Perhaps because he identified himself so closely with the tattered roustabout of the play, Robeson has consistently championed the poor and downtrodden, not only of his own race, but of every race, creed, and color. A magnificent figure of a man, he is probably one of America's best-loved leaders.

STARVATION

ALBAN BERG, the Viennese composer, star pupil of "twelve-tone Schoenberg," was in funds. His opera *Wozzeck* had been successfully performed and he was riding high. He had even bought a Ford with part of his proceeds. He was somewhat taken aback, then, to read in a local newspaper an article which reported him to be "neglected and starving." He at once telephoned a friend, called his attention to the item, and added, "Tonight we shall have to starve better than usual; come and starve with us." They went gaily out to one of the best restaurants in that city of good food, Vienna, and consumed an expensive dinner. Berg paid the check.

NO FUSS

WHEN Fiorello La Guardia was mayor of
New York, he never missed a concert if he
could help it. The way to his heart was
through the baton, for there was nothing he
liked better than to lead an orchestra. When
he was invited to conduct the band of the
New York Fire Department in a gala concert at Carnegie Hall, he accepted with
alacrity.

The director of the hall, wishing to make
this a very special occasion, hired extra ushers
and spotlight, and planned a souvenir program. When La Guardia got wind of the
preparations, he sent for the director. "Please,
no fuss," he begged. "Just treat me as you
would treat Toscanini."

◈◈◈◈◈◈◈◈◈◈◈◈◈◈◈◈◈◈◈◈◈◈◈◈◈◈◈◈◈

ERNEST SCHELLING'S
VICTORY BALL

WORLD WAR I was over. The historic railway
coach at Compiègne had witnessed the signing
of the armistice. The peoples of the world
heaved a sigh of relief that wafted their spirits
as high as they had previously been low. Almost at once, big celebrations were planned.
Balls and parties became the order of the
nights; a craze for dancing swept the war-
weary countries.

A young English poet, Alfred Noyes, was
invited to a fashionable ball in London. As
he watched the whirling dancers and listened
to the blaring band, he thought grimly of
those who had died that these might dance.
He pictured their resentment at the apparent
frivolity and heartlessness of the dancers.
Lines of poetry came into his head:"

"Shadows of dead men grin by the wall,
  Watching the fun of the Victory Ball."

At home, later, he wrote his poem, and
called it *The Victory Ball*.

When Ernest Schelling read Noyes' poem, he was deeply impressed. He had served with the armed forces, and had seen enough of death and desolation to realize the meaning of the poet's words and to resent, with him, the apparent disregard by the living of the dead. So he made a musical setting of the poem, a dramatic piece of program music that made its point unmistakably. Between the rhythms of one-step, fox-trot, waltz, and tango, he interpolated trumpet signals, national airs, a call to arms, the crescendo march of an approaching army, the sound of a plane. The Hymn of Death (Dies Irae) and "Taps" at the end silence the dance music, and the Victory Ball ends quietly, on a note of sadness. Thus Schelling reproached the thoughtless in music, as Noyes had in words.

FOUR MEN IN A DILEMMA

WHEN THE FAMOUS Flonzaley Quartet was on tour in America in the 1920's, they stopped off to play a concert in a Middle Western city which shall be nameless. Some of the leading citizens came to call during the day before the concert, and one of them expressed a wish to hear the Brahms C-Minor String Quartet, a work seldom played at that time. "If only I could hear the Flonzaley Quartet play it, I'd die happy," he said.

"Gladly," replied Adolfo Betti, the first violinist of the quartet. "The piece is in our repertoire, and I'd be delighted to put it on the program. Only I do not have the music with me, as we were not expecting to play it on this trip."

"If that's all, don't give it a second thought," said the visitor. "I'm an amateur violinist myself. I own the music, and you are welcome to it."

"Good. In that case, we'll play it."

"I will see that it is in your hands in plenty of time."

The man was as good as his word. An hour or so before the performance, a package of music came by special messenger to Mr. Betti's hotel, and he explained to the others that it was to be the last piece, the grand finale, and that they should put everything they had into it, to make it an extraordinarily fine performance.

All went smoothly at the concert. At last it was time for the Brahms; a special announcement to the audience preceded it. The music was placed on the stands, the opening chords rang out, rich and full, for a while all proceeded magnificently. Then something went wrong. First the second fiddle, then the cello, then the viola started to play notes never in that place in the score. Mr. Betti glared with his one good eye at each offending player in turn, the mistake was rectified, and the performance continued. Not till they were halfway through, when he turned a page in his own part, and found that he had turned two, did he discover the trouble. The music was brand new, the pages had never been cut! His players had been obliged to "compose from memory." They got through the piece quite creditably, all things considered, but Mr. Betti had lost ten pounds and added ten years before the end was reached.

SO MANY PEOPLE!

THE PIANIST MOSZKOWSKI, hospitable to the nth degree, found himself seated at his lunch-table one day, surrounded by fifteen friends, who had drifted in and whom he had invited for luncheon. Presently, a solitary little thin-breasted chicken on a large platter was brought in and placed with a flourish in the middle of the table. As Moszkowski related the story, he said, "The chicken raised itself on the platter, looked around the table, murmured, "Que de monde!" (So many people!), and subsided despairingly.

It may have been at that very luncheon that, when the sparse meal was over, the host said jovially, "This has been very pleasant. Let's do it again." (Recommençons.) "Oh, let's do it again right now" (Recommençons tout de suite), retorted a hungry guest.

SECURITY

LEONARD BERNSTEIN WAS rehearsing the New York Philharmonic Orchestra for a concert in what he humorously called the "Even Stephen" series (second and fourth) as distinct from the Odd Fellows (first and third). The work was unfamiliar to him and to the players, and required close concentration. Bernstein never scolded the men in rehearsal, but appealed to their musicianship to do right by the work in hand. At the end of the rehearsal, he went over to the trombone players, looking as worried as though he had failed in an exam. "Did I give you boys a wrong cue?" he asked anxiously. He hadn't, but he was quite ready to apologize if he had. Commented one of the "boys" afterward, "A conductor who isn't afraid to admit that he might have goofed! Brother, that's security!"

"There isn't anything musical Bernstein can't do," he added, "except sing, and he even tries to do that. And what a memory!

One day in Tanglewood, he and Aaron Copland went for a walk. They chatted about everything and nothing, and on the way back, Copland said, 'Well, Lenny, we've talked a lot but I bet you that neither of us can remember a word of what we've said.' What'll you bet,' said Bernstein. And he recited the entire conversation word for word, backward as well as forward."

◇◇◇◇◇◇◇◇◇◇◇◇◇◇◇◇◇◇◇◇◇◇◇◇◇◇

CORPORAL PUNISHMENT

THE COMPOSER SAMUEL BARBER was a corporal in the Army Air Corps during the Second World War. His Second Symphony, dedicated to the Air Corps had its première in 1944. After the performance, Barber received a "fan" letter from a Chinese fellow-corporal. It read

"Dear Mr. Barber,

I came to hear your symphony. I thought it was terrible, but I applauded as hard as I could because I think all corporals should be encouraged."

ELMAN VERSUS HEIFETZ

As a SMALL child, the violinist Michael Rabin was taken to Mischa Elman for the great man's opinion of his talent. He played well, and Mischa nodded approvingly and patted him kindly on the head. "Well, my boy," he said, "I suppose that when you are grown up, you will want to play the violin in an orchestra, like your father."

"Oh no, Mr. Elman," protested the boy. "When I'm grown up, I want to be a great violinist like Mr. Heifetz."

A companion story has to do with a young admirer who approached Mischa after a concert, begging him for an autograph, if possible on a photograph. Elman then said genially, "Haven't I seen you before?"

"Yes," replied the boy, "I was at your last concert and the one before."

"Delighted," beamed Elman, and signed his name with a flourish.

"I'm collecting your autographs, Mr. Elman," said the boy.

"That's very nice," approved Elman.

"You see," continued his fan, "I have a friend who collects Heifetz. He offered me one Heifetz for three Elmans."

THE PEPPERY
SIR THOMAS BEECHAM

SIR THOMAS BEECHAM was to conduct *Louise* at the Met, and Grace Moore was to sing the title role. They had not met, but both had heard things about each other and were all set for mutual dislike. The manager was so afraid of spontaneous combustion between them that he arranged to play the piano accompaniment himself for the rehearsal. Everyone was onstage, waiting for Grace Moore. Pinza was roaming up and down, reporters and photographers, Sir Thomas, everyone but Miss Moore. Finally, she arrived, heavy-eyed, looking very much like the day after the night before. She started by refusing to pose for the waiting photographers, and the rehearsal was called to order. At one point, Sir Thomas corrected her, and she rapped out haughtily, "I know this role."

So the rehearsal proceeded, tense and unsatisfactory. A coffee break was called. Beecham reminisced genially about other performances of *Louise*. There was one, he said, in which he had had to correct the tenor frequently. "And I did correct him," he said, with a sidewise glance at Grace Moore. "The tenor didn't like it a bit. He complained, "But Mr. Beecham, the soprano dies too soon." And do you know what I told him? I told him, 'My dear Sir, no soprano ever dies too soon.'" In the burst of laughter that followed, Grace Moore had to choose between slapping his face and taking her medicine. She decided to laugh, and the rehearsal continued in an atmosphere of sweetness and light.

◇◇◇◇◇◇◇◇◇◇◇◇◇◇◇◇◇◇◇◇◇◇◇◇◇◇

THE TACTFUL BRAHMS

WHEN JOHANNES BRAHMS had become a successful composer, leaving the poverty of his youthful days behind him, he naturally wished to share his affluence with his father. But Brahms père was not at all cooperative. In fact, he consistently refused his son's offers of financial support.

One day, Johannnes said to him, "Father, I have found that music comforts me in every situation as nothing else does. Whenever you feel discouraged or low, and need something to cheer you, you just take down my score of Handel's *Saul,* and read it through. I'm sure you will find in it what you need."

When Brahms Senior was browsing through the library a few days later he recalled his son's words, took the score of Handel's *Saul* from the shelf, and leafed through it. He did find exactly what he needed, for between each page, his son had inserted a bank-note.

◇◇◇◇◇◇◇◇◇◇◇◇◇◇◇◇◇◇◇◇◇◇◇◇◇◇

HOFMANN SAVED THE DAY

AT ONE of Josef Hofmann's piano recitals, he played a composition by his friend and colleague, Anton Rubinstein. After the concert, Mrs. Ernest Hutcheson, the wife of another colleague, rushed into the green-room and embraced him enthusiastically. "Oh Josef, what you do to that piece!" she crescendoed. Hofmann retorted grimly, "God knows, **I had to. Rubinstein didn't!"**

THE RETORT COURTEOUS

MARY GARDEN was wearing a strapless evening gown in the days when that was a daring thing to do. An amorous old gentleman kept his eyes glued hopefully on Mary's white expanse of bosom. Finally he could bear it no longer. "What keeps your dress up, my dear?" he asked. "Only your age, sir," retorted Mary.

DEFLATED

THE PIANIST De Pachmann returned from a worldwide tour, bursting with self-esteem. He had cried "Gut, De Pachmann," aloud to himself many times, at many different pianos. He was his own best audience. "I had a succès fou," he told his friend Moszkowski. "Crowded houses, lovely ladies, big parties, mad enthusiasm. And furthermore, how much money do you think I made?" "Half," sourly replied his friend.

STOKOWSKI WAITED

ONE DAY IN 1920, when both Leopold Stokowski and Igor Stravinsky happened to be in Berlin at the same time, Stokowski decided that he really should call and pay his respects to the Russian composer who, rumor said, was contemplating a visit to the United States. He accordingly presented himself at the door of Stravinsky's hotel room. He knocked. The door was opened a crack. Oeberg, Stravinsky's publisher, peered through the crack." "Well?" he said. "And what do *you* want?" "I want to see Stravinsky." "He's taking a bath. I'm waiting to see him myself." "Please tell him I'm here." Oeberg called in Russian, "Hey, Igor, there's a guy here who wants to see you." "Tell him to go away and come back another time," splashed Stravinsky in the same language. "He says he's the conductor of a symphony orchestra in America," yelled Oeberg. "Ask him what orchestra." "He says the Philadelphia Orchestra." "Never heard of it," bellowed Stravinsky. "Never heard of a place called Philadelphia.

Never heard it had an orchestra. He's an impostor. Send him away."

Stokowski, who spoke Russian, understood every word that was said. He had been getting madder and madder. "Wait a minute," he interrupted. "There *is* a town called

Philadelphia, it *has* an orchestra, I *am* its conductor. What's more, I'll prove it!" He shifted from one numb leg to the other. "I'll go to my hotel and get some recordings. We'll see who's an impostor." He came back within the hour, with a satchel full of records. Even then, he was not admitted, but was obliged to pass the records through the door, while he waited outside. Stravinsky played a half-dozen or so before, at long last, he finally admitted Stokowski. Not until he was sure that there was an orchestra, that it was good, and that Stokowski was its conductor, did he relent so far as to open the door.

PROKOFIEFF THE TRUTH-TELLER

WHEN OLIN DOWNES asked the blond giant
Prokofieff, a Russian visitor to the United
States in the 1920's, who, in his opinion, were
the most important living Russian composers,
he replied forthrightly, "Stravinsky, Myself,
and Miaskovsky." Characteristically, he
put himself where he honestly thought he belonged—neither first nor last. A truth teller,
he saw no reason for beating about the bush.

At an earlier stage in his career, when he was
a student at the Conservatory of St. Petersburg, he spoke the truth equally bluntly. He
attended a concert given by Rachmaninoff,
friend and admirer of the recently deceased
Scriabin, over whose open grave the pianist
had vowed a series of concerts devoted to
Scriabin's music. The occasion was an emotional one for him. As Prokofieff wandered
about the lobby during the intermission, he
heard many disapproving remarks about the
performance. The intelligentsia of St. Peters-

burg let fly against the pianist's failure to grasp
the "profound, recondite, inner mysticism"
of Scriabin. (It is questionable how much they
themselves grasped.) Prokofieff disagreed
with them silently. He liked the music, felt
that it had been interpreted well and movingly.
Afterward, he barged into the greenroom,
shook hands with the artist. "Your performance was not bad at all," he assured the great
man. "Really not bad." (He was actually
replying to the critics, unknown to Rachmaninoff.) "How dare you? What do you
mean, not bad?" thundered Rachmaninoff,
incensed at the impudence of this whippersnapper. He glowered and turned his back
on the impertinent youngster. Prokofieff left.
That was the end, for the time being. It was
not until years later, when they met over a
chessboard, on an ocean liner, that all was
forgiven, and the two men became friends.

RHAPSODY IN BLUE

"A CONCERT in which classical music is jazzed, and jazz classicized! Now *that's* something new under the sun," said band-leader Paul Whiteman. "I'll try it." He engaged New York's Aeolian Hall for Feb. 12, 1924. He ordered new Tuxedos for his band. And, most important, he commissioned young George Gershwin, a successful song writer then in his twenties, to write something new for the concert.

Gershwin was game, but scared. All he had written to date were singable songs. But he composed the *Rhapsody in Blue* for piano and orchestra by the sweat of his brow. Then he found he couldn't bear to part with it. Whenever Whiteman asked him for the score, he begged off. "Just a few more days," he pleaded. "I have to make some changes."

Time rolled around to a week before the concert, and still Gershwin pored feverishly over his manuscript. Whiteman sent messengers to pick it up. They returned empty-handed. Finally, he went himself. He placed his three hundred pounds of avoirdupois in Gershwin's most comfortable armchair, turned a deaf ear to Gershwin's pleas and excuses, and refused to leave until the score was in his hands. The composer finally had to give in, and Whiteman departed in triumph with an envelope almost as fat as himself.

"Damn the fool! Did he actually believe he could improve on it?" was his verdict after rehearsal—a mixture of jubilation and incredulity. And audiences since then have agreed with him one hundred percent.

SWEET-SCENTED *PARSIFAL*

KARL MUCK was conducting a rehearsal of *Parsifal* in Bayreuth. A sweet young thing from Alabama, attending the rehearsal, murmured rapturously, upon the entrance of the flower-girls attending Kundry, "Oh, I do love the flower-girls. I think they're so *seducive*." Meanwhile, the maidens were singing, "Ich dufte süss, Ich dufte süss" (I smell so sweet, I smell so sweet.) Muck rapped peremptorily on his music-stand, turned to the flower-maidens. "Unfortunately," he said, "I am too far away to be a good judge, but I do know that you are smelling sweet a quarter-note too soon."

OPERATIC DUEL

THE OPERATIC TENOR Lauritz Melchior, and
the soprano Maria Jeritza were singing together in Wagner's opera, *Die Walküre*. He
was Siegfried, she was Sieglinde. Came the
moment when she sank at his feet, and lay
supine while he delivered an impressive aria.
She fell. She lay for a moment. He started
his aria. In her, ambition reared its ugly
head. She could not allow him to have the
lime-light. With a Wagnerian kick, she
thrust aside the flowing white draperies of
Sieglinde, revealing one of the most approved
pairs of legs on the operatic scene. As she
anticipated, all eyes were turned to the unexpected display. Melchior sang a few measures to an inattentive audience. He looked
down, grasped the situation. With a vicious
kick, he restored the draperies to their initial
classical perfection, not hesitating to include
the leg with the draperies in his gesture. But
Jeritza was not thus to be deterred. Again

she threw them aside for the delectation of the multitude, again he replaced them. The duel continued to the end of the scene, to the fascination of the audience. Result—a draw.

RAVEL'S *BOLERO* BY TOSCANINI

WHEN TOSCANINI and the Philharmonic Orchestra were touring Europe, Paris was one of the high spots of their tour. There they gave the first performance of Ravel's *Bolero*, the piece which later aroused American audiences to wild enthusiasm.

The Maestro had his own idea of how the *Bolero* should be played. It could be an exciting piece, and he sensed its possibilities. His conception embraced a fast tempo, an urgent crescendo, a whispering pianissimo at the finish. That was the way he felt it. That was the way he rehearsed it.

Came the evening of the première. By a slip-up, Ravel, the composer, had not received a "courtesy" ticket for the performance. Naturally, he was angry at the oversight, but he wanted to hear the great Toscanini play his piece. So he pushed and shoved like any American football player into the crowded hall. He arrived just as the first strains of the *Bolero* were sounded. In a bad mood to

start with, he was furious when he heard
Toscanini's interpretation of his piece. It
was too fast, to him unbearably so. (In the
recording, his own tempo is deliberate to the
point of dullness.) It was too this, it was too
that. Audibly and unfavorably, he lashed out
criticisms of tempo, interpretation, and mood,
much to the annoyance of the Parisian audience, enthralled by Toscanini's performance.
They saw in Ravel, not the composer (they
didn't recognize him), but an annoying crank
who was spoiling their fun. They shushed
him.

After the performance, Ravel, distracted,
hastened to the artists' room to tell Toscanini
what he thought of him. He stamped his
feet, waved his arms, danced about. "The
Bolero is a dance," he cried. "But not a fast
one. It does not call for a speed-up such as
you have given it. Slower, it must be slower."
The Maestro, unaccustomed to being hauled
over the coals in this fashion, was intrigued,
but firm. In his mind, that was the way the
Bolero should sound, that was the way he
intended to continue playing it—and did.
A comparison of his recording with one of
Ravel's is all that is needed to demonstrate
their respective effectiveness.

As a sequel to this story, there is the tale of
the downfall of the snaredrummer Schmehl,

a member of Toscanini's orchestra, over this same *Bolero*. The snare drummer's delicately beaten crescendi and diminuendi were vital to the effectiveness of the piece. Schmehl did his best, and it was very good. After several successful performances, Toscanini called a meeting of the members of the percussion section, and took occasion to single out Schmehl for special approbation. "Thanks, Boss. Glad you feel that way about me," was the casual response. But Schmehl was by no means casual about praise from hard-to-get Toscanini. Inwardly, he was in a dither. Suppose he couldn't continue to play his part as the Maestro liked it! What then? Self-consciousness overcame him. Suddenly he couldn't relax. He forgot what it was he had done that had so pleased the Maestro.

The next time the orchestra played Ravel's *Bolero*, Schmehl was in a panic, completely unaccountable. He began his opening solo *forte*, instead of *piano*. Toscanini glared at him and muttered bad words in Italian under his breath while furiously beating time. Schmehl's partner suggested in a low voice that he take the sticks and play the part until the unhappy drummer had come to himself. Schmehl was too far gone in panic to follow the suggestion. He continued drumming away *forte*. A sympathetic trombone emitted a loud blast instead of a quiet tone at the climax of a solo. From then on, the *Bolero* was confusion worse confounded.

When the last chord was reached, after what seemed an eternity, Toscanini hurried from the stage without a glance at the audience, without acknowledgment of the applause. In his room, he cried, "Where is Schmehl? I want Schmehl. Send me Schmehl!" Eventually Schmehl, apologetic, shame-faced, hangdog, appeared. He wanted to explain all. But he never had a chance. "Stupido, salud, you play no more for me!" was the Maestro's opening line. He went on from there. Schmehl's fighting spirit was aroused. The Maestro had praised him extravagantly only a short while ago. Surely he didn't deserve the torrent of abuse being showered upon him now. He blinked. After forty years in an orchestra he was prepared to receive criticism, but finally he could take no more. With a shrug he retorted, "You don't like my work? All right. So get yourself another boy." And Toscanini did.

CON ESPRESSIONE

At a rehearsal one day, Toscanini noticed that a violinist he had recently engaged was looking far from happy. The man played well, drew his bow correctly enough across the strings, observed the dynamics, followed the beat, but all with an air of lacklustre boredom. The maestro had never seen such a thing in an orchestra led by him. He felt himself challenged. He conducted even more painstakingly than usual, put his best foot forward. Special fire went into every dramatic moment, special passion wherever it was indicated. Still, there was no evidence of interest or emotion on the "dead pan" facing him. The man appeared ready to burst into tears of sheer ennui, and between numbers, remained seated, neutral and inert, without uttering a word, without even smoking a cigarette.

During an intermission, Toscanini could stand it no longer. He went over to talk to this strange individual. "What's the matter?" he asked. "Don't you like the pieces we've been playing?" "They're all right."

"Well, then, perhaps you don't care for the way I conduct them?" "It's all right." "Would you prefer to play first violin instead of second?" "This is all right." "In heaven's name, then what is wrong with you?" "Nothing, maestro. It's just that I don't like music anyway."

TOSCANINI AND THE
ETERNAL FEMININE

WHEN FRANCES ALDA was twenty-three years old, already a spoiled darling of the opera at Covent Garden and Parma, she was summoned to La Scala to sing the title role of Charpentier's *Louise*. The great Toscanini was to conduct. She studied the part carefully and duly appeared in Milan for her first rehearsal.

Gatti-Casazza, manager of La Scala and her devoted friend (he afterward married her) was there, off in a corner. Toscanini sat beside the pianist, immobile, eyes closed, only a finger raised now and again to indicate tempo. Alda gulped, opened her mouth, sang the whole role straight through, as she had learned it. No word from Toscanini. The pianist struck the final chord. Still—silence. Then Toscanini leaned over the pianist's shoulder, closed the score on the rack. In a voice of dulcet charm, and in Italian, he inquired blandly, "Tell me, in what language were you singing?"

Alda burst into tears, refused to answer him. Who was he to criticize her Italian accent, which had got by in the past without difficulty? She flounced out of the room, back to the Hotel Milan to have a good cry. Gatti was much upset. He sent flowers, apologies, entreaties to her room. She tore up his notes, refused his apologies, damned his La Scala. She was ready to quit. Then Gatti wrote her that Toscanini would go through the score with her word by word, teach her the perfect pronunciation, if she would come to him. Meekly, she went. She knew on which side her bread was buttered.

Once Toscanini mimicked her pronunciation of a word. She stopped singing. With flashing eyes she said in French, "I must tell you, Maestro, if you do that just once again— just once—I shall walk out of here." And Toscanini, who had replied previously to an irate singer reminding him that she was a star and would brook no correction, "Madam, I know no stars excepting those in the heavens," Toscanini, who was later to smash a valuable wrist watch in a temper at his N.B.C. orchestra men—Toscanini bowed his head, and took it from little Frances Alda.

GENIUS VERSUS TALENT

THE DETERMINED MOTHER of a wonder-child assailed the great conductor Toscanini by letter, telegram, and telephone until he consented to grant her an audition. Promptly at the appointed hour she arrived, leading the lamb to the slaughter. Everything proceeded according to form. The child took out his violin and played his little piece, the Maestro listened in silence. The silence continued after the music had ceased. Finally, unable to bear it any longer, the mother exploded, "Well, Maestro, don't you think my son is a genius?" "A genius, Madam? I don't know. But I can assure you that he has no talent."

On another occasion, however, when a grown-up listened to a wonder-child, the joke was on him. Toscanini was dial-twisting at the radio one evening in his home, when a phrase from Beethoven's Seventh Symphony caught his ear. He listened approvingly. "I wonder who is conducting," he remarked to his wife. "Whoever it is, he reads it admirably. Just listen to this." As the symphony went on, he waxed more and more enthusiastic. "I couldn't do it better myself," he remarked. When the announcer came to the microphone, Toscanini learned that he had been listening to a recording by the New York Philharmonic Orchestra, with Arturo Toscanini directing. Talent? No. Genius!

CAN'T YOU COUNT?

ARTUR SCHNABEL, famous Viennese pianist, was spending a quiet evening in 1938 at home with Albert Einstein, father of the theory of relativity, and probably the greatest mathematician in the world. As usual, Einstein brought out his beloved fiddle, spread a Mozart Sonata on the rack (literally), and prepared to enjoy himself. He invited Schnabel to join him in making music. Also as usual, Einstein's performance was far from perfect. Schnabel loved Einstein dearly and he suffered in silence. He stopped occasionally to let him catch up, and controlled his irritation with the amateur's difficulties sufficiently to try to explain them away. But his slim stock of patience became exhausted. Finally, as Einstein played raptly on, with partly closed eyes and a sublime disregard of the requirements of tempo, Schnabel banged out a few arresting chords. And he cried aloud in his pain—the pianist chiding the mathematician —"No, no, Albert. Can't you count? One-two-three-four, one-two-three-four."

UNEXPECTED

JUST AS THE musical Lieblings sat down to dinner one evening, the door-bell rang. "Your friend, Mr. X, is here," announced the maid. "Dear me, how very inconvenient! Show him in the living-room, and ask him if he'd mind waiting," said Mr. Liebling, annoyed at the interruption. The family dined in leisurely fashion, and then Mr. Liebling, full of dessert and good will, went into the living room. "Well, well, my friend," he said genially, "awfully sorry to keep you waiting. But we always dine punctually at seven." "That's what I thought," retorted X drily. "In fact, that's what you told me when you invited me to dinner tonight."

HINDEMITH'S *MATHIS DER MALER*

IN 1939, Paul Hindemith arrived in New York, a small blond man, laden down with musical instruments of various descriptions. A viola d'amore and a viola dangled from either hand, and others loomed in the background, mingled with trunks and suitcases. On the dock in the H section, a tough Irish customs inspector assigned to examine his luggage glared at him in a fashion hardly reassuring to a visitor on visa. As the inspector became aware of the musical instruments, the glare softened perceptibly. "Say, do you play?" he asked. "Well, yes." "Do you know Heifetz?" "Kind of," modestly. "Do you know Serkin, Busch, Rubinstein, Szigeti, Lotte Lehmann?" "I sure do." The inspector whipped out his chalk, marked all of Hindemith's baggage with the cabalistic symbol that passed it through the gates, without opening a lid. "Let him in," he barked. "He's all right." In he came.

He brought with him not only the instruments he played, but an opera he had composed. Back home, in Germany, he had completed a musical setting of the life of Matthias

Grünewald, a medieval painter. Grünewald, known not only as the painter of the Eidesheim altar, but as a leader in the 14th century Peasant Revolt, had achieved a delayed renown. Some incidents in his life captured Hindemith's imagination. The composer took time off to go and live in the monastery near Mainz associated with the painter-monk. There he remained for six months, steeping himself in Grünewald's atmosphere and studying Grünewald's life. Hindemith became more Grünewald than Grünewald himself during those six months. He emerged from seclusion prepared to write an opera, and shortly thereafter completed *Mathis der Maler*.

Mathis der Maler was banned from Germany as "Kulturbolshevismus" and its composer was pronounced a Kulturbolshevist. Blond Aryan though he was, Hindemith bowed to the interdiction. He told American reporters plaintively, "You can search me why they called my music degenerate. I suppose because it is modernistic." He quit Germany and went to Switzerland, with *Mathis* as a traveling companion. The opera was produced in Zürich in the May preceding his arrival in this country. Parts of it have been performed here by symphony orchestras and it will doubtless be produced in its entirety as an opera in the near future.

THE CONSIDERATE
CONDUCTOR

FRITZ REINER was on the podium, with raised
baton, ready to conduct a final pre-concert rehearsal of Strauss's *Till Eulenspiegel*. Glancing
toward the brass section, he noticed that the
first horn player was not the man he had
previously rehearsed. As there are many difficult horn passages in the composition, he
thought it best to make some inquiry. "You
have, of course, performed *Till Eulenspiegel?*"
he asked. "Nope." "You have undoubtedly
heard the work?" "Nope." "Well, I hope
you will enjoy it," said Reiner, and gave the
signal to commence.

BLOOD, SWEAT AND TEARS
—AND A SYMPHONY

IN A DINGY, three-a-day movie house in Leningrad, a shabby youth sat before an equally shabby upright piano. In the dim light, he peered short-sightedly through horn-rimmed glasses at the narrative score propped on the piano, telling the story of the picture flickering on the screen, while his fingers mechanically thumped the keys descriptively, tenderly, ferociously, or unobtrusively, as the score demanded.

Had young Dmitri Shostakovitch had his choice, he would certainly not have elected to spend his spare time in this fashion. To go from the Leningrad Conservatory, where his teacher Nicolaev thought so highly of his talent as to teach him gratis, to the drudgery of this job, was a severe strain, not only on his resolution but on his health. The atmosphere was stifling. Two stoves kept the temperature well over 90°, and caused a perpetual steam to rise from the snowy clothing of the audience. When the doors were opened, icy draughts penetrated into every corner, and **Dmitri** would blow on hands which, a moment before, had been hot and damp with perspiration. After the last performance, dressed only in a thin overcoat, without gloves or galoshes, he would stagger home at one A.M., only to repeat the dreary round the following day.

When, under such conditions, he can have found the time to work on his *First Symphony*, is a mystery. Poverty and misfortune were the cradles of his inspiration. He was in constant dread of losing the piano on which he practiced at home, and indeed he did lose it for a while because he could not keep up the payments. He fell ill, and the family was deprived of even the few roubles he earned. His mother had been working to repay a sum of money stolen, through no fault of hers, from the cash-box of her employers. She was beaten and robbed of the money when she had almost achieved her goal. The family was practically starving.

And yet—Dmitri wrote his First Symphony! Somehow, he finished it. And somehow, he humbly brought it to Nicolaev for critical advice. Nicolaev approved. So, too, did the Conservatory authorities for after examining the work, they agreed to pay for the copying of the orchestral parts, a prohibitive expense for Dmitri.

All of this took months. Meanwhile, his health improved, so did his fortunes. Then he was chosen to represent Leningrad's young composers at a conference in Moscow. Here he stepped out, not as an adolescent movie pianist, but as a mature young man, one to be reckoned with. He was respectfully listened to, was wined and dined, and—most important to him—was promised that his symphony should be published after it had been performed. He left Moscow, walking on air.

Having returned to Leningrad and survived what he described as the "hellish work" of correcting the orchestra parts, he prepared happily for the performance of the symphony. It took place on May 12, 1926, and was immediately successful. The following year he was commissioned by the Soviet government to write a second symphony, in commemoration of the October revolution. Shostakovitch had come of age. At twenty-one, a battle-scarred veteran, he took his place as a full-fledged Soviet composer.

ABSENT-MINDED

GRADUATION exercises were in process at the Eastman School of Music in Rochester. A program of compositions by contemporary Americans, many of them Eastman alumni, was wending its weary way toward the moment when diplomas would be distributed. Alec Wilder, a graduate of the school and a composer of jazz and serious items which had arrested critical attention, dozed in his seat. An hour of atonality, polytonality, cacophony finally reduced him to dreamless slumber.

A song roused him. He liked it thoroughly. "Hey, that's good!" He leaped to his feet. "Bravo, bravo," he shouted at the top of his lungs. "Encore."

The friend with him yanked him roughly down to his seat. "For the love of Mike," he said, "That's enough. Sit down. Sit down and shut up."

"Why?" demanded Wilder. "That's a wonderful song. Best I've heard in a long time."

"Sure it is, sure. But you wrote it!"

SCHOENBERG AND
THE GOOD EARTH

WHEN THE FILM of Pearl Buck's novel, *The Good Earth*, was being made, the producers decided to call in special composers for some of the big scenes. Arnold Schoenberg was in Hollywood, and it occurred to one up-to-date producer that a twelve-tone background might produce a fine stormy effect so he sent his representative to call on the composer and sound him out.

The story of *The Good Earth* was explained in detail, while the representative kept his eyes open to see if the composer's imagination took fire. But, except for an attitude of polite listening, Schoenberg did not register. Then his caller really became eloquent in describing the big scene. "Think of it," he said, "There's a terrific storm going on, the wheat field is swaying in the wind, and suddenly the earth begins to tremble. An earthquake! In the midst of the earthquake, Oo-lan gives birth to a baby. What an opportunity!"

"With so much going on," Schoenberg said mildly, "why do you need music?"

NO ACCOUNTING FOR TASTES

WHEN BÉLA BARTÒK, the Hungarian composer, was a young man, he lived for a while in Paris, the Mecca of musicians. He called on Isidor Philip, head of the piano department in the Paris Conservatoire and dean of piano peda- gogues there, bringing with him a letter of in- troduction from Busoni. Philip hospitably suggested that he present the young man to the musical celebrities of the day. "You'd like to know Saint-Saëns?" he inquired. Most young musicians would have jumped at the oppor- tunity. Bartòk shook his head. "No, thank you," he replied indifferently. "How about the organist of Saint Sulpice, Charles Marie Widor?" Bartòk again declined. "Massenet? Dukas?" Another negative response. "But since you're in Paris, you really should learn to know some of our great Frenchmen," urged Philip. "If you don't care to meet those I've named, is there anybody else—?" Bartòk's face lit up with one of his rare smiles. "Yes, there is," he replied decidedly. "Claude Debussy." "Debussy!" echoed Philip. "Well" (doubtfully), "if you like, I will go with you when you call on him. He is rather unapproachable, and moreover a pretty unpleasant person. He hates most people, and will assuredly be rude to you. Do you want to be insulted by Debussy?" "Yes," said Bartòk simply.

◇◇◇◇◇◇◇◇◇◇◇◇◇◇◇◇◇◇◇◇◇◇◇◇

CHILD PRODIGY, PRODIGIOUS CHILD

WHEN GEORGES ENESCO, Rumanian composer-violinist, was a child prodigy of five, he was taken to see a great teacher of the violin.

"Well, my little man," said the Maestro condescendingly, "suppose you show me what you can do."

"Not until you have shown *me*," retorted the fiery little boy.

He firmly refused to play until assured by the teacher's performance that he could rely upon his musical judgment.

TREASURE TROVE IN
THE KREMLIN

WHEN THE TIDE of war seemed about to sweep
the German army into Rumania during World
War I, the composer Georges Enesco was advised to flee to Moscow for safety. He packed
his belongings in haste. Into one valise went
the precious manuscripts of his unpublished
second symphony, his second suite, piano
quartet, and others.

"But you cannot take your manuscripts to
Russia with you," protested the Rumanian
foreign minister Duca, Enesco's good friend.
"They will surely be declared contraband, and
will be confiscated at the border."

"What shall I do then?" asked Enesco.

"Let me take charge of them for you. I
will send them with other valuables to London
for safe-keeping."

Reluctantly, Enesco uncurled his fingers
from the handle of the valise and with a sink-
ing heart saw it carried away, to be placed
with the Rumanian court jewels, gold reserve,
and other treasures. His forebodings were

justified. The consignment never reached
London. Reports placed it now here, now
there. At last, ironically enough, its travels
were halted in Moscow. Enesco, of course,
knew nothing of this. He had meanwhile decided to remain in Bucharest, the threatened

invasion not having materialized at that time. He gave up his valise and its contents for lost.

The Russians, however, displayed excellent judgment. They confiscated as a prize of war all articles of intrinsic value. The music they declared to be harmless and without monetary importance, and returned it to the valise, which was placed in one of the vaults of the Kremlin for safekeeping. There it lay, gathering dust. For six years, Enesco heard nothing of it.

In 1924, when he was concertizing in New York, a cablegram was handed to him as he was leaving the house en route to an engagement. He stuffed it in his pocket, to read later. On the subway, he took it out. When he read it, a delicious tremor shook him from head to foot. It told him that his manuscripts were safe, that they were in the Kremlin, that they would be returned to him. He was deliriously happy. His friend, Duca, was later assassinated by the Germans, but his music had lived.

To this day, he is grateful to the Russians for sparing his brain-child. When he visited Moscow in 1946, the Second Suite was performed in his honor. It elicited a chorus of approval from Soviet musicians, from Shostakovitch up and down. They felt a proprietary interest in it, as well they might.

COPLAND MARCHES ON

A GANGLING YOUNG MAN of eighteen sat at the piano in the concert hall of the music school for Americans in Fontainebleau. The occasion was a students' concert, the date about 1918. To Aaron Copland, it offered an opportunity to play for an audience a piano piece he had written back home, called *The Cat and the Mouse*. His teacher in New York, Rubin Goldmark, had said he had "no criteria to judge such music," and had frankly not liked the piece, but Aaron still did. It pleased the students. While the concert was still being applauded, a Frenchman came back-stage, presented Copland with his card, and asked the young man to come to see him. When Copland saw the name on the card, he nearly fell over. It was Durand, a name well known to him as the publisher of Debussy's music. He lost no time in calling at the publisher's office. And when he was offered twenty-five dollars for *The Cat and the Mouse*, as outright payment for all rights for all time and all countries, he gratefully accepted the offer.

As it turned out, this was probably the least astute business deal he ever made. The piece became a hit which coined money for the publisher, while the composer gained only renown. He never committed that error again.

He went right on composing. When he returned to America with his organ concerto, he was already vaguely known as a composer of works that were wild and woolly, judged by the standards of the 1920's. A flabbergasted audience heard Nadia Boulanger play that organ concerto with Walter Damrosch in New York. Damrosch's dignified conducting of the orchestra was reassuring, but his own response was not. Nadia Boulanger, who had taught Aaron in Paris and believed in him, had pressured Damrosch into playing Copland, by herself refusing to play anything else. But the conductor took revenge. In the bewildered silence that ensued after the performance of the concerto, Damrosch turned to the audience, and announced in his sonorous voice, "If a young man at the age of twenty-three can write a symphony like that, in five years he will be ready to commit murder."

Copland went right on composing. He became better and better known. In the late 1920's, he wrote a concerto for the piano, containing some elements of jazz. It automatically was christened *Jazz Concerto*. After the first New York performance he was invited to California, to play it in the famous Hollywood Bowl. When he arrived in Los Angeles what was his astonishment to see, in the middle of the Union Station, mounted on a platform, a piano. He blinked. A huge crowd milled about it. Press photographers and reporters were on hand, with plenty of flash-light bulbs and typewriters. A press-agent informed him that this had all been planned for him, and that he was expected to sit right down at the piano and play jazz. He blinked again. For Copland doesn't, never has, and never will, play jazz in the Hollywood sense of the word. And so the jazz-hungry crowd was sent away unsatisfied.

Copland goes right on composing. Ballets, a children's opera, Mexican pieces, film music, supplement his growing output of serious works. He is probably, according to a recent poll, the best-known composer writing in America today. And he marches on!

◇◇◇◇◇◇◇◇◇◇◇◇◇◇◇◇◇◇◇◇◇◇◇◇◇◇◇◇◇

THE UNPREDICTABLE IVES

IN 1947 CHARLES IVES, who has slowly come to be recognized as one of the most original and forward-looking of American composers, was awarded the Pulitzer Prize for his *Third Symphony*. This is an honor not to be taken lightly. The fact that it came to Ives thirty-nine long, toilsome years after he had written the symphony is understandable. It is, in fact, more understandable than the symphony itself, which contains complexities too difficult for ordinary ears. Ives, a very retiring gentleman, had no pleasure in the award, which he had never sought. When his friends came to see him after hearing the news, he refused to accept their congratulations.

"Such prizes are the badge of mediocrity," he stated.

FAUX PAS

THE SISTER OF Jascha Heifetz, who is an excellent pianist but a shy person, was invited with her husband Samuel Chotzinoff to a dinner in honor of the great physicist Dr. Albert Einstein. "Please don't seat me near Dr. Einstein," she said to her hostess. "I honestly wouldn't know what to talk to him about."

The hostess promised. But by some last-minute shift in arrangements, the place-cards were changed about, and to her dismay, Mrs. Chotzinoff found herself at table beside the great man. She was completely tongue-tied. Dr. Einstein started a conversation by asking, "Tell me, what is your main interest, Mrs. Chotzinoff?"

Forgetting that Dr. Einstein played the violin, remembering only that he was the world's greatest mathematician, she blurted, "Geometry, I like geometry."

"Plane geometry?" he inquired with interest.

"Why?" she replied. "Is there a fancy?"

TRISTAN PLUS

THE OPERA WAS Tristan and Isolde, Act II.
Melchior and Flagstad sat on their garden
bench, pouring out their love in sweet strains
of highly premeditated art. The scenery had
been freshly painted, the luminous moonlit
sky of the Met's best backdrop had never
glowed more romantically, the audience
looked and listened with a sense of deep en-
chantment.

Suddenly a swinging platform appeared
from nowhere against the blue sky. It descended slowly, majestically, propelled by in-
visible machinery. On it were seated four
men in shirtsleeves, playing poker. So ab-
sorbed were they that they failed to notice
their surroundings. As stagehands, ascend-
ing and descending were all in their day's
work. They did not look up until the laughter of the audience broke into a roar. When
they realized where they were, they had
themselves whisked up faster than they had
come down. But the scene was spoiled. It
would have taken a more powerful love
philtre than the one administered to the lovers by Brangäne to recreate its magic.

HEFTY CONTRALTO

MADAME SCHUMANN-HEINK the singer was
so well upholstered that she often found herself going through doors sideways in order to
get by. She was engaged to sing a concert in
a small midwestern town. When she arrived,
just before the concert, she was dismayed to
find that she had to ascend a wobbly flight
of steps to a wobbly stage, which shook with
every footstep. With fear and trepidation,
she made her deliberate entrance and sang
her program straight through without an intermission. At the end, the applause was
hearty. She turned to go out for the usual
exit before encores. But instead of leaving
the stage she simply turned her back to the
audience and waited for the next round of
applause. Then she faced about, smiling her
widest, and in her broad German accent announced "I don't go. I t'ought maybe you'd
vant me back, I should some encores sing."
She was taking no chances.

TANGLEWOOD TALE

AN ENTHUSIASTIC MEMBER of the audience at a Tanglewood Thursday evening concert went backstage to congratulate the conductor on his fine performance and was graciously received. On the following Saturday, there was another concert, and again she appeared in the green-room. "Maestro, this was the most beautiful concert I ever had the privilege of attending," she exclaimed.

To which he replied sharply, "So? And what was wrong with last Thursday's concert?"